If Women *Ruled the World*

HOW TO CREATE THE WORLD WE WANT TO LIVE IN
— Stories, Ideas, and Inspiration for Change

Edited by Sheila Ellison

Inner Ocean Publishing Inc.
Maui, Hawai'i • San Francisco, California

Inner Ocean Publishing, Inc.
P.O. Box 1239
Makawao, Maui, HI 96768-1239

Printed on recycled paper

Cover and book design by Maxine Ressler
Illustration by Jane Evershed

PUBLISHER CATALOGING-IN-PUBLICATION DATA
If women ruled the world : how to create a world we want to live in
: stories, ideas, and inspiration for change / edited by Sheila Ellison.
— Makawao, HI : Inner Ocean, 2004.
p. cm.
Includes index.
ISBN: 1-930722-36-2
1. Women's studies. 2. Social sciences. 3. Social change.
4. Women—Quotations. 5. Women—Anecdotes.
HQ1180 .I49 2004
305.4—dc22 0410

DISTRIBUTED BY PUBLISHERS GROUP WEST

To all women everywhere,
those who fight for equality
and those whose voices have yet
to be heard. Together we have
the strength to spark change.

Contents

Foreword by Marie C. Wilson

Often in my work, I hear people say that the lack of women in leadership is an issue that pales next to world crises—global terrorism, fragile economics, inadequate health care, access to quality education, corporate greed. They see no connection between the frightening situations we're in and the fact that few women sit at the table to determine the solutions. No wonder we're where we are today.

This fundamental imbalance, with men running the world and women mostly spectators (or victims), is not a trivial detail. It *is* the problem. It is also the one solution we have not tried and the one most likely to work.

First of all, to counter those who think women actually *do* run the world, I offer a few statistics from my own backyard: The United States is 57th in the world in women's political representation (behind Slovakia and tied with Andorra); the pipeline to political leadership in America, the state legislatures, has been hovering at about 20 percent for a decade; men occupy 86 percent of Congressional seats, 84 percent of governorships, and 88 percent of the seats on top corporate boards. Yet women are more than half of the U.S. population. And the numbers get worse when we examine the diversity of women at the top, especially when you consider the enormous population growth in communities of color.

It is shocking and inspiring to hear how "developing" countries continue to rocket ahead of our pillar of democracy—limited in financial resources, they certainly know how to use their human resources. Last year, The White House Project organized two major conferences where women from around the world tutored one another on how we might bring each other closer to democracy. It was energizing to consider the potential, and saddening to remember how many years—and how many great leaders—have passed without change.

One woman, a majestic member of the South African Parliament, upon hearing of our nation's failure to trust women with real power and authority, stood before the crowd and promised to stand by her sisters in America as we fight for our rightful place in control of our destiny. I could have cried. I think of her offer to help as I travel across the nation, promoting women in political and business leadership. I also remember the words of the women of France and India and Sweden and Switzerland—democracy without women in power is not democracy at all.

But forget fairness for a moment. It's not that putting women in power is simply the right thing to do—it's the *only* thing to do. The values that women uniquely bring to the table—empathy, inclusion across lines of authority, relational skills, community focus—are vital if we are to solve any of the monumental issues facing our world today. This is not just me talking. Three decades of research in state legislatures, universities, and international public policy centers have proven beyond doubt that women, children, *and* men all benefit when women are in leadership. Broader societal legislation, benefiting everyone, is more likely to pass if women are in office. We know the power of women as peacemakers in the world from scores of stories about their effectiveness at negotiation, from South Africa to India to Pakistan to Ireland and beyond.

We can ill afford to use only half our talent, when we know for a fact that complicated challenges demand more than one vision. It's time for real and permanent power sharing, for real and permanent change—

women ruling side by side with men, allowing their voices to rise with different solutions and allowing men to think outside of the masculine box. In this way, we get fresh eyes and fresh solutions from both genders, applied to both old and abiding problems and to new and frightening ones.

This is not a call to pry power from the fingers of men and turn it all over to women. Together we can create a different world, shifting the burden from male shoulders and allowing the diversity of thought and life experience to transform our solutions—perhaps bringing a greater peace, perhaps allowing men to be better fathers, perhaps providing a new paradigm for our security.

It's not easy to get there. Those in power rarely let go without a fight, even if they would benefit by doing so. For women to truly gain the leadership roles we deserve, we must be insistent and persistent. We must enlist our many male allies. We must step up to the plate, letting it be known that we are ready to lead, that in fact we demand it as a birthright. If we think creatively, if we use our community resources (a particular strength of women), if we support women who say they want to lead, if we use our voices and our votes to get there, we will sustain the transformation of power. And everyone will be better for it. Our daughters and sons and grandchildren will thank us, because their world will offer more options. We owe it to them. And to ourselves.

Marie C. Wilson is founder and president of The White House Project (www.thewhitehouseproject.org), a national nonprofit organization dedicated to advancing women's leadership across sectors and fostering the entry of women into all positions of leadership, including the U.S. presidency. She is also the author of the new book *Closing the Leadership Gap: Why Women Can and Must Help Run the World.*

Introduction

Never doubt that a small group of thoughtful,
committed citizens can change the world;
indeed, it's the only thing that ever has.
—Margaret Mead, anthropologist

As the editor of this moving collection of essays, I had the honor of meeting many women, of hearing their stories, and of being moved to tears over their struggles: women still suffer from violence in their homes, still feel powerless over the influence of cultural traditions, and continue to be passed over for promotion because of parental choices. Not to mention some less vexing troubles that made me laugh: difficulties overcoming an obsession with ice cream, accepting our thighs, and setting boundaries with our mothers-in-law.

The title to each essay completes the sentence that begins with "If women ruled the world." The goal of this book was to gather stories and experiences from all areas of our lives, from the everyday struggles of child care, body image, family life, and sexuality to the bigger challenges confronting the world like media violence, global warming, and world peace. We wanted to hear from women who already held leadership positions as well as from women who haven't had the opportunity to be publicly heard, from women who might not identify themselves as politically active, who haven't had the chance to write a book, or chair a conference, or run a nonprofit. We accomplished that goal by setting up a Web site that asked women to answer the question, "If women ruled the world, what would it be like?" Over a two-month period we received 13,000 hits and hundreds of essays from women of every background—with and without kids, old and young, from those who had a humorous experience with the issue they wanted to address, to those whose words screamed of injustice, inequality, and world problems so big that I would set the essay aside and stare at my computer screen, unable to move, unsure if the world was actually ready to hear truth behind the words. What moved me most was how alike we are. Regardless of upbringing, economics, or education, underneath the skin of women is a wild, protective, nurturing strength that knows we're in trouble. We know somehow we have to rise together and take a stand. We may disagree on the direction society needs to move in, but we all agree it needs to get moving! The willingness of women to speak their truths, to step forward with creative solutions, and to take the time to engage in the process renewed my hope.

I learned that you, too, see a new world rising from the ashes of mistakes, poor choices, and lack of direction; you believe that women have the ability, compassion, determination, and courage to take the steps needed to create the changes we all want to see in our world. We unanimously agreed that leadership—nurturing, healing, awareness, all the names you gave to '*ruling*'—must begin within ourselves. Without an understanding of our potential and the courage to take responsibility for our choices at the most basic levels of self, family, and community, we won't gain the skills or confidence to share the power, lead the people, or make changes on a national or world level. How can we stop a war if we haven't achieved peace in our own homes, with the people we love? How can we save our environment if we're afraid to mention recycling options to a neighbor who wheels three trashcans to the street each week but has no bin for bottles and cans? To begin any process, you have to start somewhere, and although it's easier sometimes to point our fingers outward at all the problems that plague our world, it's most productive and satisfying to start with the areas where we already have the most influence. For that reason, this book is divided into sections, starting with the personal and moving outward in a circle that grows larger as more people and issues are added—beginning with self, expanding to family, embracing community, then going outward to include business and national issues, and finally ending with how we can create a better world.

The truth is that many of the topics in *If Women Ruled the World*—from body image to shared parenting to women in leadership positions to world peace—have been on our social and personal radar for 30 years. We may feel dissatisfied, conflicted, furious, resigned, or even inspired to take action—but the fact remains: We're still dealing with some of the same issues. Many women are still afraid to take charge; we apologize for choices we make, feel guilty when we put ourselves first, and at some level may even believe that women aren't meant to rule. I received many fearful notes from both men and women, questioning the title of the book, afraid that we were suggesting a female takeover. They said, "Women shouldn't rule; rather, we should nurture or cooperatively share the power." Maybe so, but to get to a place where we are equally sharing the power, we have to assume more leadership positions and believe we have the determination, intelligence, and compassion to rule at all levels.

Throughout my life I've been involved in social issues; my parents made sure that our family volunteered in soup kitchens, camps for disabled kids, community cleanups, and programs for the homeless. In college I spent a summer volunteering in Poland and years as a youth director at an inner-city church. All of these experiences were one-on-one interactions with people who needed help; they were community-based and helped me to understand my parents' words: "If you've been given much in life, you must give something back." Once I married and had four kids of my own, I had less interest in what was going on around me; my world consisted of my home, my family, my friends, my husband's success and what that bought for us. If you had asked me about world hunger or the Cold War—the issues of the day—I would have had a vague bad feeling but not much more.

But then my life changed dramatically: I was suddenly a single mother of four children with no financial support, and my youngest son was diagnosed with autism. My awareness skyrocketed: the challenge of paying the rent, the high cost of health care, the inadequate choice of schools, and the lack of career options for a woman who'd spent ten years raising kids propelled me into action. I realized that, although I'd never considered myself political, there were now issues I was dealing with every day that were being decided through our political process. In small and large ways I was already an activist: when I went to the school district explaining the laws that protected my son's rights, when I helped single mothers find free court services, when I wrote a letter to the paper about education cuts or sent an e-mail off to my representative. When asked to edit this book, I first responded, "You need to get someone with more political experience." To which my publisher responded, "No, we want someone who lives with the consequences of the political process, who understands firsthand what health care or gun violence or religious intolerance means." Women understand community; we see an issue and we respond; we volunteer and help those in need—our lives are touched daily by some political policy or another.

I'm a woman just like you, juggling a life, carrying others along on my journey, wishing for peace, envisioning a world where love rules and hoping that many of the topics discussed in this book will be non-issues when my daughters reach middle age. I want my grandchildren to look up at me and say, "You mean there was a time when a woman was not president!?"

The intent of this book is to engage your mind, heart, and imagination to the point where you feel uniquely called to participate. It's time to transform our anger and complaints into action, which is why we included a call-to-action idea after many essays. You'll also find interesting sidebars, which were added to give more information on the topic, to offer historical facts, interesting resources, and a touch of humor. We hope to raise awareness of issues around the globe, where some kind of change, redirection, or creative solution is desperately needed. A chorus of voices is what we're striving for, so you may not agree with every idea, which means you'll be challenged to think—why don't you agree, what do you think would work better, and how would you confront the issue? Change is about movement, and movement in any direction is impossible without an idea. Being afraid to rule is no longer an option. Start in your backyard and take it out to the streets. As an old saying goes, "To the world you might be just one person, but to one person you might be the world."

We already rule more aspects of our lives than we think; the time to embrace that power is now.

—Sheila Ellison

The Courage to Be Ourselves

Section 1

Be yourself. The world worships the original.

—Jean Cocteau, writer

Introduction

We Would Trust Ourselves

Lisa Loeb, singer-songwriter

I grew up in Dallas, Texas, in the 1980s, a conservative time, in a fairly affluent part of town where people were very well groomed. There was a sense of security in having your hair done, your lipstick on, your nails manicured, and your clothes stylish and tidy, almost more so than having your thoughts in order and your opinions developed. As a young girl, I sometimes felt that there was too much emphasis on the outside and not enough on the inside. This made me uncomfortable, yet somehow, fulfilling the basic expectations of society made fitting-in an easy process, by simply checking items off of a list or following a book of rules.

When I arrived at Brown University, I felt slightly relieved. I was finally in a place that valued creativity more than fitting in. I realized that my reservations about placing so much emphasis on what everyone else thinks were based on some truth—I could feel much more like myself when I no longer had to waste so much time on those superficial things.

This made it easier for me to write and explore my creative expression as a musician. In fact, I wrote a song freshman year with lyrics that said, "Don't be afraid to be yourself, you'll get nowhere being someone else, and if you do, it really won't be you going somewhere." This was a revelation: that you really only succeed if you act like yourself; otherwise, it's as if it's not you at all.

As a songwriter, I'm often asked for advice by young musicians, and I've realized that the best thing I can do is to encourage them to find their own voice, musically and lyrically. If they concentrate on fitting-in, they'll lose the only thing that really sets them apart from others—their individuality.

Don't get me wrong; I do think that there's something to empathy, and to respecting and understanding society's values and the community's expectations, but one must also trust oneself and one's own inner voice. Even now, I'm sometimes faced with making decisions about inane subjects such as which outfits I'll wear in certain situations. A short skirt at a work-related meeting with men? Hmm. No, that might give them the wrong idea, or it might make them even more interested, and I don't play sexy to get what I want in business. Deciding what to wear on stage? Well, the miniskirt is cute, comfortable, and a small item to pack in a suitcase, but a feminist writer might think that I'm not strong enough if I'm wearing a girly skirt and makeup. It can go both ways. In the end, especially with these silly superficial choices, I just go with my gut, and assume that some subtle expression of my values and myself will make my intentions clear.

Going to an all girl's school for 11 years, I had to wear a uniform, and as kids, we girls would think, "Hey, why do they want us to all look alike? Why are they taking away our individuality?" As it turns out, that was the point—to emphasize the inside. Being well groomed can give you an easy starting point for fitting-in, and there's nothing wrong with that, but if women ruled the world, we could start by focusing on the inside, and not think so hard about our choices and what they mean to everyone else.

SINGER-SONGWRITER LISA LOEB debuted at No. 1 on the charts in 1994 with "Stay (I Missed You)." She has released five CDs since, recieved two Grammy nominations and a Parent's Choice Award for her children's album "Catch the Moon."

Peace Would Begin with Me

Ultimately, we have just one moral duty: to reclaim large areas of peace in ourselves, more and more peace, and to reflect it toward others. And the more peace there is in us, the more peace there will be in our troubled world.

—Etty Hillesum, writer

Wherever I go in the world as a professional peacemaker, I always find more women ready to take on the work of peace than men. Maybe it's because women and their children account for 80 percent of the casualties of today's wars. Maybe it's because women are naturally more "relational" than men. Maybe it's because women, as givers of life, value that which sustains life over that which destroys it.

Whatever the reason, I am fascinated by how women take so readily to the understanding that "peace begins with me." I think of Rawda, a Palestinian woman who, like Nelson Mandela, was jailed by her "enemies" yet discovered in prison a commitment to come back to her community as a nonviolent peacemaker instead of an angry activist and went on to participate in and train others for Israeli-Palestinian dialogues.

I think of Katie, a Greek Cypriot woman, who nearly walked out of her first encounter with a Turkish Cypriot but stayed because she realized that if she wanted to bring peace to her island, she would have to learn to open her heart even to the ones she "hated." She went on to run dozens of bicommunal dialogue groups and started a bicommunal choir.

I think of Sonia, who survived the rape camps in Bosnia and found peace in her own heart to work with other traumatized victims.

In my own life, inner peace has been a spiritual as well as practical journey. I have a sanctuary in my imagination—a place I go to feel that deep sense of calm, that vibrant sense of being, that heightened sense of connection to all that is, which I call inner peace. I first learned to go there thirty years ago, when I had a near-death experience on the operating table, during my second radical mastectomy for breast cancer.

That experience opened the doorway to my spiritual journey and showed me that, not knowing when I would die (and having no more fear of death), I was free to choose to live my life full of peace, joy, and love. Having defied all the statistical expectations (I was in the "zero" percent survival category), I also realized I was here on Earth for a purpose—to serve humanity by calling the people home to peace.

Since then, I have learned (and taught) many skills for building peace, but the single most important one has been the ability to drop into that place of deep inner peace at will, and to amplify the energy field of that place for those around me. I have seen that practice calm trigger-happy wild young boys with AK-47s at road blocks in Liberia; I have seen it open the space for transforming tense and potentially violent confrontations into a fruitful dialogue.

I have worked with women from all over the world, and I find that they have a deep capacity for finding this place of inner peace, and from it, they're able to open their hearts to reconciliation and healing. I think it has something to do with being mothers. We carry the seeds of life to fruition. We nurture, we listen, we comfort, we maintain relationships. We are connected to our children—and to the life force—in ways that men can never be. Being closer to the cycles of the natural world, we intuitively understand when the circle of life is shattered and needs healing.

In Bosnia one day the following poem came to me:

We are broken
And we will not be mended
Until we remember
That we are unbreakable.

Women get it. And because we get it, we are the mothers of peace—from the inside out.

LOUISE DIAMOND, PH.D., is a professional peacebuilder in places of ethnic conflict around the world, president of the Peace Company, and author of *The Peace Book: 108 Simple Ways to Create a More Peaceful World.*

Self-Respect Classes Would Be Part of Our High School Curriculum

How many cares one loses when one decides not to be something, but to be someone.

—Coco Chanel, designer

While strolling through my high school's quad last week, I could not help but notice the outfits of the shivering young girls around me. "Isn't it 35 degrees out?" I mumbled confusedly to myself as scantily clad girls rushed to the nearest warm classroom. Standing there, I thought back to my freshman year, three years ago, and reminisced, "I think I used to wear outfits like that, too. What happened?" I could have walked away from that thought with a mere chuckle. But seeing the obviously uncomfortable clothing those girls were sporting got me wondering: Why?

Of course, the answer flashes before my eyes the second I turn on the TV. Music videos, with rappers "singing" about the four women they screwed last night, tell young girls only one thing: He'll like you if you're sexy.

I can remember my behavior the first two years of high school. I never expected a boy to want to have a real conversation with me. Whenever a gang of guys would approach my scantily clad self at a football game or at a dance, I acted flirtatious and coy. All I wanted was for people, male or female, to like me, so I gave up my pride and forced myself to be what I conceived to be "likeable" in dress and manner.

Luckily, a friend came into my life who taught me to have self-respect and dignity. But not all girls have been so fortunate. Now, in my senior year, I observe a few of my classmates still acting the way I once felt I needed to.

As teenagers, we're influenced by images in the media—through videos, songs, and movies—on what makes a girl sexy and how to act around guys. However, I don't think the videos, songs, and movies should stop being produced. The problem does not lie within the media necessarily but within ourselves. We need to learn and then teach our younger counterparts the art of self-respect. If women ruled, we would create mandatory classes for high school freshman girls that would teach them how to reject the promiscuous messages of popular culture. We would teach them that outer beauty isn't as important as who we are inside, and that self-confidence is more attractive than a short skirt. In these classes we could hear stories from female mentors about the choices they made regarding sex, alcohol, and dieting—and we might learn how to reject the ever-present belief that to be accepted and liked you have to act like your peers.

Just Think

Just Think envisions a country where media education is an integral part of standard education in every classroom across the United States. Their mission is to teach young people to think for themselves and to understand the words and images the media portray. They are doing their part by offering innovative media education programs and curricula to youth of all backgrounds (www.justthink.org).

If women ruled, we would teach young girls to be themselves without worrying about impressing their peers. We would teach them how to get out of frightening and threatening situations.

I am waiting anxiously for the day when my high school quad is teeming with warmly dressed, comfortable girls strolling with heads high. Until then, I will sit down with my little sister and talk to her. In doing so, I will begin to undo the mentality that pop culture has woven into the minds of American teens. I believe that is our responsibility, as women.

Janel Marie Healy, 17, is a senior in high school. Although she is still a student, she hopes to begin a career in children's literature soon.

~ *Something to Think About* ~

We Would Unlearn All That We Know

As a woman, I know how to cross my legs in a way that best hides my cellulite. I know how to best display my cleavage when I want to win an argument, get out of a speeding ticket, attract attention from a man, or avoid doing something.

As a woman, I know how to cover a pimple, how to find a swimsuit that will best cover my stretch marks, and how to remove my body hair and just accept the pain. I know that when a man gets angry, I'm to keep my mouth closed and wait for him to calm down.

As a woman, I know that my female friends will compete with me for a man's attention and my male friends will try to sleep with me. I know never to put my drink down at a party or trust any man who offers to make me a drink.

As a woman, I know that I will never be president. I know to expect to make less money than my male coworkers. I know that I will be accused of "PMS-ing" anytime I disagree with something a man is saying.

I know that I am expected to be thin with large breasts, have white teeth and clear skin, and smell like roses, *everywhere.*

If women ruled the world, we'd be raised with equal power and opportunity. Men would not treat us like objects; we wouldn't allow it. If women ruled the world, we would unlearn all that we know and learn how to love and accept ourselves, regardless of our supposed "imperfections."

—Raegan Thurlow, 24

Portrait of a Woman

The portrait of a woman
A mysterious silhouette
Artistically, so subtle
No one dares to forget

The oil on the canvas
Blends a gentle tone
Brush strokes tell a story
Of a girl who's not alone

Her eyes speak chapters
Of a fight she vows to win
Soft and flowing lines
Her mouth turned to a grin

The landscape behind her
Is filled with many faces
Distantly waiting shadows
Loving, safe embraces

Self-portrait is her duty
Only she can use the palette
A collage of several forms
Stronger than a statuette

DEANNA DAVIS operates her own child-care facility from her home and loves releasing her passionate creative side through gourmet cooking, writing poetry, dancing, and various arts and crafts projects. She is 33, a proud mother of two, and resides in Sacramento, California.

We Would Celebrate Our Strengths and Not Focus on Our Weaknesses

What are your inner gifts and talents? Most of us are reasonably articulate about our deficits and weaknesses—how many we got wrong on our spelling tests, how many things we failed to accomplish during any given day. We become fluent at explaining our incompetencies, but look straight at our gifts and talents and then mutter, "Oh, that old thing?"

—Dr. Dawna Markova, educator and writer

I was always a good student. I was able to sit and listen in classes, diligently taking notes and responding to questions. I skipped grade 8 and fast-tracked through high school. In contrast, my sister was athletic but had trouble sitting still in class, completing assignments, and listening to her teachers. School did not seem to ignite her imagination.

We both graduated and went off to different career choices. After college, I felt lost. My path wasn't laid out for me, and I found it hard to set goals and envision my future. If I was given a task, I was great at completing it, but I couldn't seem to come up with the big ideas myself. I drifted through several jobs, and my personal frustration increased. Why couldn't I seem to get it together? How had I gone from being a success in school to failing in the "real world"?

Out of school, my sister seemed to thrive. She became part of a group that went into organizations and helped them build effective leadership teams. She was great at brainstorming options and coaching people in aligning their goals within their personal and professional lives. She became the "idea" person and partnered with others in her organization who were good at procedure—so her ideas became reality.

It wasn't until I took a workshop on intellectual diversity that I learned some reassuring facts: people process information differently, and we all possess unique talents and thinking strengths.

There are people who learn by listening, people who learn by seeing, and others who learn by doing. While I could sit and listen to a teacher's voice all day, the same teacher's voice would space out my sister. My sister later found that if she was able to move around while she was listening, she could remember every word. While talking and listening made me more aware, it was movement that brought my sister into focus.

By figuring out my own learning process and then observing the way others in my life learned, I was able to change the way I interacted with people. My mother was a visual person—it was much better to write her an e-mail when we were in conflict than try to talk to her on the phone. At work I figured out that my supervisor, like my sister, found it hard to sit through long auditory presentations. To get his attention, I created more visuals and had him be an active participant.

By honoring other people's learning patterns, I became a better communicator in both my professional and personal life. I also learned to let go of the notion that we are all supposed to be good at everything. I changed my way of thinking and stopped focusing on areas I was lacking in, and instead I concentrated on the areas I was strong in. While I might not be the one to come up with the next "big idea," if I partnered with a person who did, I would be the one to bring that idea into reality.

If women ruled the world, we would embrace all of our learning diversities. If we were encouraged by our parents and teachers to identify the best way we learn and to celebrate our strengths, then we would be set up for success at an early age.

JULIE STEVENSON, 32, is an environmental consultant living with her husband in Park City, Utah.

Excellent Resources

How Your Child Is Smart by Dawna Markova and Anne Powell

Einstein Never Used Flashcards by Roberta Michnick Golinkoff and Kathy Hirsh-Pasek

Teaching with the Brain in Mind by Eric Jensen

Now, Discover Your Strengths by Marcus Buckingham and Donald O. Clifton, Ph.D.

We Wouldn't Give Our Power Away

If we go down into ourselves we find
that we possess exactly what we desire.
—Simone Weil, philosopher

Fresh out of college in the suburbs of New Jersey, I headed off to Hawaii to start my new independent life—away from my protective parents and the camaraderie of my girlfriends. I had little money and no plan. On the third day of my visit I met a wonderful man. We fell in love and instantly became partners in life. Unfortunately, I soon found out that he was addicted to drugs. As the years went by, I didn't realize that I depended on him so much that I lost myself. I lost an understanding of how to take care of myself and honor my body. I didn't believe I could make "real" money, so I relied on him financially. I spent years fighting with him, trying to change him and blaming him for our horrible life. At the time, I thought that if he got his life together, *our* life would be great—until one day it dawned on me that I had to change *my* life, if I wanted to improve my situation.

The hardest part was actually finding my own sense of self so that I could leave him. And I don't mean this in a philosophical way; I mean this in a very practical, surviving-life kind of way. The first thing I did was open my own bank account and separate our money. I took on more work. Slowly I started taking responsibility for my half of the bills. This was encouraging and gave me confidence that I could take care of myself.

My next step was finding a life outside of my relationship. In the past, I had spent my energy focused on what was wrong, dwelling on the negative. I decided this time to start with hope—with daring to dream a little dream. In my real life, crisis after crisis made me stressed, irritable, and constantly sick to my stomach. In my dream world, I felt authentic, confident, and beautiful. I danced, I pranced, and I felt happy.

I began teaching my own Pilates class. Don't underestimate the importance of physically changing how you feel, and the reverberating effects in your emotional, psychological, and spiritual worlds! When I stepped outside of my daily life within our relationship and did something healthy for me, the options that life had to offer began to materialize. In adding more classes, I developed better organizational, business, and computer skills.

The more I gained strength and confidence, the more I could see the interdependence and manipulation in our dysfunctional relationship. I had given him power over me. When I started taking steps to do things for myself, I stopped being a part of that cycle. The whole dynamic of our relationship crumbled, and I was finally able to break away.

I figured out that nobody, no matter how much I love them, can make my life what it's meant to be—only I can dream my dream and manifest my own destiny. I had to stop blaming others and do the work to create a better life for myself—one that I chose and believed in. If women ruled the world, every woman would be taught from birth that she alone has control over herself and her own destiny. That she can create the life she would like to live.

Eva Bondar, 27, is a Pilates instructor who lives with her dog, Toki, in Maui, Hawaii.

Call to Action

Combat Sexual Discrimination and Harassment

- If you think you're being harassed or discriminated against, trust your feelings. If you're still not sure, know that sexual harassment is behavior of a sexual nature that makes someone feel uncomfortable or unwelcome in the workplace by focusing attention on their gender instead of on their professional qualifications.
- Speak up at the time. Be sure to say *"No"* clearly, firmly, and without looking amused. There is a chance that the harasser does not realize the behavior is offensive, so be firm in communicating that you are offended.
- Most states have sexual harassment laws. Find them at www.de.psu.edu/harassment/legal/state.html.
- Know your rights. Sexual harassment is illegal. The Equal Employment Opportunity Commission (www.eeoc.gov) requires all organizations with more than fifteen employees to have policies and procedures to deal with sexual harassment.
- Keep records. Record what happens in a journal and keep any letters, notes, other documents, or artifacts you receive. Write down the dates, times, places, and an account of what happened. Write down the names of any witnesses.
- Identify an advocate, someone who is designated to help you use the resources of the schools or workplace effectively.

- Write a letter. People have successfully stopped sexual harassment by writing a polite letter detailing the behavior that is offensive and asking the person who is harassing them to stop the behavior.
- Report sexual harassment to the appropriate person in the organization.
- File a complaint with your state agency that deals with employment discrimination.

We'd Learn to Disappoint Others

Nine-tenths of our suffering is caused by others not thinking so much of us as we think they ought.

—Mary Lyon, founder of Mt. Holyoke College

From the time I took my first breath, I'm sure my training began in the subtlest of ways: you should be pleasing, do kind things for others, and never rock the boat, so that everyone will like you. It wasn't until I turned 34 and was miserable in my marriage that I began to question why I was making all my life decisions based on what others expected. I didn't want to disappoint my parents by announcing the first divorce in family history, and I was afraid my kids would never forgive me when I told them I couldn't live with their dad anymore. So I stayed married for many more years before I found the courage to choose myself.

To everyone I was the super mother of two, able to leap tall homework assignments and swing from sewing thread! My husband and I made the perfect couple, college sweethearts. Yet I lived imprisoned by other's expectations until the day I announced the divorce and learned that disappointing everyone wasn't as bad as I thought it would be.

In fact, the realization that my family and kids still loved me changed the way I live my life, because as tragic as the divorce was, my choice didn't change who I was in anyone's eyes. For all those years I was sure that something terrible would happen to me if I let people down.

Once I learned this freedom skill, it became easier and easier to choose myself and not care what others thought of me. I began asking myself, "What do I want?" throughout each day, and often weighed that against what my kids wanted—and said "No" to them—even when I could see the dismal response on their faces.

It's been years now, and I'm a pro at disappointing others without feeling a twinge of guilt. In the process of making this personal transformation, I've taught my children invaluable life skills. The most important is that relationships are about disappointment—you disappoint others over and over throughout life—but we still choose to love; that's what it means to be in a relationship. The second is that you can't and won't always get what you want; girls especially need mothers who model to them that it's okay to let other people down and to choose what they want.

If women ruled the world, we'd be raised surrounded by powerful women who wouldn't need to please others to get what they wanted from life.

Susan Chairo, 39, is a graphic designer, the mother of two and a professional at saying "No" as often as possible if it means gaining time to herself.

Ice Cream Would Be Considered the Sustenance of Life and Not a Guilty Pleasure

Seize the moment. Remember all those women on the Titanic *who waved off the dessert cart.*

—Erma Bombeck, journalist and author

During my high school days, I made it a point to eat ice cream as often as possible. A two-scoop minimum—no fat-free, low-fat, fro yo—just the full-fat, calorie-laden, scrumptious, velvety kind of ice cream. I loved life, I loved my body, and suffice to say, I adored ice cream. I had never thought of myself as having a "weight problem." I felt secure in my own right. I felt sexy and beautiful, and I didn't need anyone to verify this. But something happened that changed all that.

I started to look at the covers of magazines and wish that I could somehow emulate the vision of "perfection" I was seeing. I could no longer look at beauty magazines and giggle at the surrealism of the airbrushed models. I no longer ate ice cream with dinner. Actually, I no longer ate ice cream at all. I no longer loved and respected my body for what it was—my form, my unique fashion—it all seemed so insufficient.

I lost weight, and a lot of it—a total loss of about 75 pounds. Yet as the pounds melted away (in a healthy manner) over the course of approximately two years, so did my self-confidence. The more I became focused on losing weight the more I lost the capability of seeing myself clearly.

At the time I was working as a waitress. Suddenly my tips increased. I recall speaking to a cook in the back room about this strange phenomenon. He responded with, "Well, duh . . . you're taking meat off your bones. You already look a hell of a lot better, you know?"

It was at that moment when I realized that I hadn't changed, at least not internally. I was losing weight and being "rewarded" for it. After I lost 50 pounds, regular (and incredibly stingy) customers would leave me their phone numbers along with a generous tip. In fact, a former high school classmate came into the restaurant and didn't recognize me. When I reintroduced myself, he said, "I had no idea you were so pretty."

I've never felt uglier than I did in that moment. I realized that it was more important for me to feel good about myself—for myself—which meant choosing a healthier diet. I had regained my self-confidence and created a new definition of what was beautiful. I started to eat ice cream again. And I enjoyed it more than words can ever explain.

The moral of my story is that ice cream is merely an analogy for living life to the fullest, for indulging yourself simply because you're fabulous . . . just as you are. This means eating that piece of cake because you want to and not feeling the guilt of calories and fat grams or the pressure of society to obtain and remain at a less-than-healthy weight because "thin is in." It means feeling secure and confident in your own skin, embracing your luscious curves, and seeing yourself as

By the Numbers

- The average American model is 5 feet 11 inches tall and weighs 117 pounds. The average woman is 5 feet 4 inches, weighs 140 pounds, and wears a size 14, according to Eating Disorders Awareness.
- Americans spend more than $40 billion a year on dieting and diet-related products. That's roughly equivalent to the amount the U.S. federal government spends on education each year.
- 80 percent of 10-year-olds are dieting.
- 89 percent of women are dissatisfied with their bodies.

the sexy woman you are, no matter what size jeans you wear. What could be more delicious than that?

COURTNEY A. FITZGERALD, 23, is a graduate student at Governors State University, currently pursuing her second master of arts in communication studies; her B.A. and her first M.A. are both in English. She currently resides in Crestwood, Illinois.

~ Something to Think About ~

WHAT "YOU" THINK ABOUT ME

It didn't happen overnight. It took me 50 years to discover that what I had been searching for all my life in other people was right here, deep within my very being. For much of my life I wanted to be you; I wanted to have what you had, buy what you could afford, and be just that: *You.* I didn't have a clue that what I had been searching for most of my life was deep inside. I just didn't recognize her. "You" are that person who has no bearing on where I am going with my life today, for "You" no longer exist for me. At one time, long ago, "You" were all I had. Today, I have Hope. Hope and those around me who respect what I stand for and the choices I make, and those gifts of rediscovery I pass to women who still sit and still listen to "You."

—Shar Dirkovich, 55

We Would Love Our Thighs

I think the quality of sexiness comes from within.
It is something that is in you or it isn't and it really doesn't have much to do with breasts or thighs or the pout of your lips.

—Sophia Loren, actor

Our culture is gripped with thigh anxiety. Seventy-two percent of American women polled say they wish they had "better" thighs. Liposuction has become the most requested cosmetic surgery procedure in the country. Before 1973, dimpling of the thighs was considered natural, even female. Then the word *cellulite* was not only introduced to the vernacular by *Vogue* magazine, but listed as a "disfiguring" problem. American women, who now spend more than $100 million a year on thigh-reduction products, have been plagued with worry and shame over cellulite ever since.

I count myself as one of them. I do love living in my body; I feel deeply at home inside my skin. But even after years of body-awareness work, when I catch a glimpse of my thighs in a mirror, or see them spreading out against a chair, part of me cringes inside. I know it's ridiculous, this cultural brainwashing about thighs, but I have to admit that I've been affected by it.

If women ruled the world, *cellulite* would not be a word in our vocabulary. Liposuction would not be a routine procedure. We would not feel that our thighs needed to look like those of the models we see in magazines or on commercials, plucked clean and sleek as the plastic-wrapped chicken thighs at the supermarket. Naomi Campbell has stated publicly that she has cellulite, but it is always airbrushed out of her photos. I think it would do great things for the self-esteem of women in our culture if her image wasn't airbrushed. It would be even better if airbrushes didn't exist at all, if we could see ourselves, our own real female bodies, represented regularly on the page and on the screen.

An Alarming Trend . . .

According the American Association of Plastic Surgeons, 8.7 million plastic surgeries were done in 2003, up 32 percent from 2002. Twenty-six percent of these surgeries were performed on people between the ages of 19 and 34.

A friend of mine recently saw a movie in which a beautiful woman was not airbrushed. The actress was naked; some cellulite was dimpling her rear. My friend said that time stood still for her as she watched that scene. She looked at that cellulite and couldn't see anything else on the screen. She was flooded with gratitude. Here was a real body. Here was a body like hers. And the woman was still attractive, still sexy; she wasn't diminished in any way because she had a few ripples on her thighs, her bum. She became even more sympathetic as a character, more human.

I have a vision of women and girls of all ages, all sizes, parading down a street. Our thighs are bare—our big thighs, skinny thighs, veined thighs, scarred thighs, our lumpy thighs, hairy thighs, marbled thighs, muscled thighs, our warm, alive thighs. No one is looking on in judgment. No one is catcalling or hooting or heckling. No one is saying, "Cover those things up!," and no one is thinking, "My thighs are so gross," or "I bet everyone is looking at my cellulite," or "If only I lost 10 pounds . . . ," or "I hate my legs, I hate my legs, I hate my legs." All of us are walking, or maybe running, or dancing. All of us are appreciating the power of our own legs, appreciating the power of one another's legs. We can almost hear that power as we continue on our path—the sound of our thighs thundering.

GAYLE BRANDEIS, 36, is the author of *Fruitflesh: Seeds of Inspiration for Women Who Write* and *The Book of Dead Birds: A Novel.* She and her family live in Riverside, California.

Labels Wouldn't Define the Woman

In America, money takes the place of God.

—Anzia Yezierski, novelist

Have you ever thought about how the world would be if we all dressed the same? How about this: cashmere and cotton robes. Cashmere or cotton underwear, bras, cotton briefs and boxers. All white. Rubber sandals and lambskin boots. All black. If I ruled the world, these would be the only items of clothing people could place on their bodies.

What would the Country Club Mothers of America do without their Lacoste? What would the Upper East Side teenagers in New York do without their Manolo Blahniks? What would the Beverly Hills girls do without their Sevens? What would the angry teenagers of America do without their black trench coats? And what the hell is Britney Spears going to do to entertain us now? I can't wait to see.

Perhaps they will all stampede through the country like a wild herd, scrounging the land, searching endlessly for something else that could outwardly show whatever it is that they want people to believe about them. Maybe skin branding would become popular, so people can have "Sexy" or "Slutty" or "Boring" or "Cheap" or "Rich" or "More Rich" printed right there on their foreheads. Perhaps everyone would begin to carry around pictures of their homes just in case they forget during the day that they are indeed happy and successful. Maybe gym memberships, diet pills, eating disorders, and obesity rates would plummet, with people losing interest in their perfectly toned bodies. Instead of shopping on the weekends, families would have more time to spend together.

If I ruled the world, clothing wouldn't mean so much. It wouldn't have implication, status, attractiveness, or judgment sewn so seamlessly throughout. If women ruled the world, the labels on my clothes would not be the sole symbol of who I was as a person. Labels wouldn't define the woman. Instead of looking at fashion magazines, wishing for clothes we can't afford to buy, we could spend our time enjoying our bodies and our lives—maybe learning a new hobby or hiking with a friend. Maybe we'd write poetry or find time to help the homeless. We would care more about developing our inner selves than adorning our bodies.

Vanity Sizing

Size tags on more expensive clothing are often reduced (a practice called "vanity sizing") to encourage women to cough it up in order to "fit" into a smaller size.

BROOKE ELLISON, 17, is a freshman at the University of Colorado, Boulder, and is an aspiring novelist.

CALL TO ACTION

Get Behind Good Labor Practices

Support companies that treat their workers fairly. Consult one of the organizations that deal specifically with labor issues:

- The National Labor Committee (www.nlcnet.org)
- Amnesty International (www.amnesty.org)
- The Worker Rights Consortium (www.workersrights.org)
- Sweatshop Watch (www.sweatshopwatch.org)

Everyone Would Explore Gender and Sexuality Freely

What is important now is that we free ourselves from the prison of gender.

—Carolyn Heilbrun, writer and social critic

I count myself lucky to have discovered that I was attracted to women. No one ever suggested I consider the possibility.

The idea that I could respond to women astounded me. So did the concept that I could be sexy as a tomboy or a butch or an androgyne, not just as a glamour girl. As I came out to straight friends and family, I discovered that many of them had felt some same-sex attraction in their lives. When I described myself as "not a boy or a girl but an elf," many laughed and admitted that they, too, felt both masculine and feminine.

If women ruled the world, I believe we would all question our sexuality and gender openly, without pressure as to the outcome. We would celebrate attractions to men and women and all combinations of maleness and femaleness. My ideas about such a world are based on vast generalizations. Still, I suspect that as people shed the unconscious fear of being queer, they might be able to enjoy some of the best aspects of queer culture.

When I was straight, I was tolerant of queers but afraid of getting too close to other women. A friend invited me to hear her play French horn in the Gay and Lesbian Pride Parade and joked that I better be careful, because girls might flirt with me. I shuddered and declined. My girlfriends and I never hugged. I looked at other girls' earrings and soft hair and curves with feelings of envy and competition instead of open admiration and desire. As far as I can tell, straight people are often consciously or unconsciously afraid that they might be queer. The fear limits friendships. Queers, however, don't need to hold back.

A Step Ahead

The International Gay and Lesbian Human Rights Commission (ILGHRC) has mobilized an unprecedented campaign to support passage of the Resolution on Sexual Orientation and Human Rights during the 2004 United Nations Human Rights Commission session. Referred to as the "Brazil Resolution," it represents the strongest and broadest message to date in support of the human rights of lesbians and gay men (www.iglhrc.org).

Queer men can be intimate with each other as friends, and not only through sports, work, or intellectual debate. They can kiss in greeting when they meet for dinner. Queer women can embrace their friends wholeheartedly, not quickly and lightly. Why shouldn't all people enjoy this warmth?

The queer community has imagined many ways of breaking out of rigid male/female roles and the power dynamics that go with them. While queers are still affected by the notions of gender they grew up with, they can explore these with a sense of play and theatricality. They can be nurturer and nurtured, strong and vulnerable, princess and cowboy, mother and father. They can adopt traditional roles with a sense of choice, not compulsion. Or they can abandon gender roles altogether. Fundamentally, queer people get to imagine what it means to be male and female for themselves. Why shouldn't all people get to claim their own gender and decide its meanings?

It is difficult and frightening to explore desire and gender in isolation. In a truly feminist society, support would be offered as a matter of course and without pressure or judgment. Sex education curricula could suggest that questioning is part of coming of age, not something abnormal that one should be ashamed of. One acquaintance of mine—a middle-aged, mostly straight woman from Wyoming—sighed when I said this. "That will be the day! But I would like to see the day when an adolescent girl in Wyoming can question her sexuality without being labeled."

The day might come, if we open up and explore our complex, beautiful capacities for love, desire, masculinity, and femininity.

ANNA MILLS, 28, tutors writing at a community college in San Francisco, California. Her work has appeared in *Bitch*, *Moxie* magazine, SoapBoxGirls.com, and *Lodestar Quarterly.*

~ Something to Think About ~

EMOTIONAL INTELLIGENCE

A couple of days ago I got upset. I don't remember what it was about, but the worst part was that I proceeded to get really upset . . . about being upset. I berated myself, rationalized, and pointed accusing fingers at myself because of the way I was feeling. If women ruled the world, maybe emotional understanding and intelligence would become part of the educational curriculum and children might discover how understanding their emotions could help get them through the stormy seas of life. We'd certainly have fewer adults sitting in therapy rooms trying to uncover long-held feelings of guilt, abandonment, anger, fear, sadness, and betrayal. We would not berate ourselves for getting upset!

—Jennifer Norris, 34

CALL TO ACTION

Combat Hate

There are many things you can do to fight hate and intolerance in your neighborhood and the world, from speaking up to lobbying local politicians to understanding the root causes of hate. Go to www.tolerance.org to see what you can do.

We Would be Sexual Dynamos

Sex is an emotion in motion.

—Mae West, actor

I dream of a world where women embrace their sexuality and revel in its power. In my fantasy world:

Women love their bodies. We are no longer slaves to an unattainable ideal for feminine beauty. Sexy images of women of all sizes and shapes are reflected back at me everywhere I look—in advertising, on TV, at work. My daughters never hear adults or peers complain about the size of their bellies or the shapes of their butts. Plastic surgeons go out of business because women are content with the wrinkles in their brows, the thinness of their lips, and the shape of their labias. Female celebrities are free to let their bodies blossom. No more actresses drop three dress sizes in order to cross over into superstardom. I never again have to read a magazine article about fad diets, colonic cleansings, diet pills, liposuction, or bodies exercised into submission. Older women get great parts in movies, and are depicted as sultry, seductive sirens rather than old maids or sexless grandmas, because age is a sign of sexual maturity and experience.

Porn reflects women's true experience of sex in all its diversity and no longer revolves around homely men ejaculating on busty porn stars. It's not about the degradation of women. It's not about violence. Instead, women's orgasms are front and center, foreplay and genuine chemistry are crucial, and hunky famous actors cater to desirable starlets (who are flashing the breasts they were born with). Women directors get the acclaim they deserve, and everyone is well paid and absolutely loves their jobs.

Women's libidos are free from medical scrutiny. Nobody is trying to sell me libido-enhancing pills, no one is measuring my sexual performance by counting notches in the bedpost, and Oprah does a show not on female sexual dysfunction but on female sexual vitality. Women are happier and hornier than ever because they have the energy and the desire to have sex. That didn't come from a pill but from having someone to help with the household chores, plus subsidized day care, universal health care, gender parity, longer vacations, and partners who've been taught how to turn us on.

Sex education prepares us for a lifetime of good sex. Because kids are taught about their bodies, including their sexual anatomy, at a young age, they are neither ashamed nor embarrassed by them. Young adults learn about sexual responsibility and respect for partners; as a result, teen pregnancy rates and disease transmission plummet to record lows. Sexual diversity is celebrated and sexual technique is taught, so that we enter adulthood with the confidence and the knowledge to embark on a lifetime of great sex.

That's not too much to ask, is it?

ANNE SEMANS is the author of *The Many Joys of Sex Toys* and the coauthor of *Sexy Mamas* and *The Good Vibrations Guide to Sex.* She lives in San Francisco with her two daughters, and she does a lot of dreaming.

Excellent (R-rated) Resources

www.cleansheets.com: A quality sex zine, part erotica/part commentary

www.clitical.com: Great resources, an active community, and a site run by a charming Webmistress—who is also a mom

www.scarletletters.com: High quality erotica, articles, and advice from a women-run site

www.janesguide.com: Jane reviews hundreds of adult sites, provides consumer tips, and exposes fraudulent practices

www.susiebright.com: Susie's site features excerpts from her sex-positive articles and essays

The Title "Sexy" Would Take Some Years to Earn

Being a sex symbol has to do with attitude, not looks.
Most men think it's looks; most women know otherwise.

—Kathleen Turner, actor

The topic of female sexual maturation has forever fascinated me and has compelled me to interview many of my female role models in their forties and fifties about their sexuality. Across the board, every woman I quizzed insisted that I hadn't experienced anything near my orgasmic potential yet. "Just wait until you hit forty," they'd say, "then you'll really fly out the roof!"

When I was younger, I didn't have the confidence in myself to communicate my needs and to ask for what I wanted. As I've grown into my skin and gotten to know my body, I've gained a powerful ability to manifest my sexuality in more internal ways. I am now able to stand tall and proud and unapologetically in my sexual power, like a queen.

Women do not come into their full orgasmic potential until they near their forties. If women ruled the world, the title "Sexy" couldn't be earned until this time of life, when women confidently know themselves and own their sexuality. And, when a woman finally did reach these orgasmically activated years, she would then and only then be revered, coveted, treasured, and pursued for her lavish and deeply erotic feminine gifts.

If women ruled the world, this entrance into our sexual prime would be celebrated and ritualized. Women at this age would be exalted. These women would be our sexy role models, appearing in print and on film, creating anticipation in every girl that one day she too would get to grow into her sexuality and be honored. Girls and young women would spend their early years learning the intricacies of their female anatomy, meanwhile gaining confidence, understanding, and an ever-increasing capacity for sexual pleasure instead of buying into antiquated expectations or social pressures about sex.

In this female-founded world, as a woman's age and sexiness quotient rose, she would become increasingly sought after for her wisdom, knowledge, confidence, and beauty in every area of her expertise. Deeply feminine sexiness would be recognizable by the beautiful lines of life drawn on a woman's face, the fullness of her belly and hips, her riveting stare, her sultry slowness, and her ability to stand still confidently, letting her presence emanate. A woman inspires. A woman mesmerizes. A *woman* is sexy.

Feel-Good Findings

In a study by Euro RSCG Worldwide, "Five Trends Shaping the Future of the Cosmetics Industry," the agency found that women today are just as interested in feeling good—physically and mentally—as they are in looking good.

The report states, "(Aging women) will have an impact on how society defines beauty."

RACHEL CAPLIN, 35, is founder of CurvOlution Size Acceptance Movement, inspiring girls and women to stop obsessively struggling to change their bodies and learn to love and accept the ones they have.

Menopause Would Be Celebrated as a Gift

We turn not older with years, but newer every day.

—Emily Dickinson

As I neared my 50th birthday, I began asking, "What is this journey my body was taking without my permission?" It came with a *rush* of energy and feelings at a level I had not experienced before. I felt drawn to the pool, so I began to swim laps as the energy began to release itself. Still full of energy, I found myself walking, running, finally arriving back at my room and falling into a restful sleep. Society called it depression, disease, inappropriate behavior.

I was overwhelmed with emotions and passionate to find out more about this "disease" they called menopause. I did not accept the medical description, which referred to all the symptoms as problems, but instead I looked for ways that I might empower myself with this energy, rather than disguise it with drugs or push it away. My heated, sweaty body awakened me many nights. Frustrated with not being able to fall back asleep, I asked myself, "Why not get up and do something?" I began to journal, paint, and garden in the early hours, and I realized that perhaps this experience was a gift.

Years went by, and I found myself about to celebrate my sixtieth birthday. Friends asked how I wanted to have a "Crone Ceremony," to celebrate my conscious decision to embrace my age with dignity and to honor my wisdom. It was another major shift for me. A newfound strength arose; I was ready for my new challenges as a Wise Woman. I had no idea how empowering it would feel to have a ritual celebrating this rite of passage.

Every woman will have an opportunity to enter menopause, with either the mindset that she has a problem that needs to be fixed or the resolve that this is an opportunity to acknowledge, embrace, and accept this gift of energy. If women ruled the world, menopause would be celebrated as a gift.

CAROLYN ANN MULCAHY, 60, is the founder and director of a menopause connection for women called Gifts of Menopause. She has two grown children and two grandsons who celebrate her wisdom.

It Only Gets Better with Age
In a 1998 Gallup survey, more than half (51 percent) of American women between ages 50 and 65 who had reached menopause said they were happiest and most fulfilled at this stage of their lives, as compared to when they were in their twenties (10 percent), thirties (17 percent) or forties (16 percent).

WAITING

You keep waiting for something to happen,
the thing that lifts you out of yourself,

catapults you into doing all the things you've put off
the great things you're meant to do in your life,

but somehow never quite get to.
You keep waiting for the planets to shift

the new moon to bring news,
the universe to align, something to give.

Meanwhile, the piles of papers, the laundry, the dishes, the job—
it all stacks up while you keep hoping

for some miracle to blast down upon you,
scattering the piles to the winds.

Sometimes you lie in bed, terrified of your life.
Sometimes you laugh at the privilege of waking.

But all the while, life goes on in its messy way.
And then you turn forty. Or fifty. Or sixty. . .

and some part of you realizes you are not alone
and you find signs of this in the animal kingdom—

when a snake sheds its skin, its eyes glaze over,
it slinks under a rock, not wanting to be touched,

and when caterpillar turns to butterfly,
if the pupa is brushed, it will die—

and when the bird taps its beak hungrily against the egg
it's because the thing is too small, too small,

and it needs to break out.
And midlife walks you into that wisdom

that this is what transformation looks like—
the mess of it, the tapping at the walls of your life,

the yearning and writhing and pushing,
until one day, one day

you emerge from the wreck
just as you are,

no, even better than that
because you know it now

both the immense dawn
and the dusk of the body

and it's all still there,
glistening and new.

Leza Lowitz, 41, is an award-winning writer, editor, and translator of Japanese who has published 11 books, including *Yoga Poems: Lines to Unfold By.* She lives in Tokyo and runs Sun and Moon Yoga.

We'd Embrace the Feminine Face of Spirituality

As truly as God is our Father, so truly is God our Mother.

—Julian of Norwich, 1373

When I was younger, it didn't bother me that here in the West the deity is most often referred to as "God the Father." My nonchalance at this gross exclusion of my gender in the Judeo-Christian religious worldview should have made me madder than hell. After all, I've got great feminist credentials. I went to Smith College back in the late '70s—and I'm old enough to have seen for myself that women can do anything they damn well feel like. It's just that until I contemplated creating a new life, it didn't dawn on me that our universe shouldn't be solely run by a single dad.

Don't get me wrong—dads are great, but mothers are also great. And since none of us would be here without one, it's more than strange that we females wouldn't have a recognized role in the cosmic creative process. After all, except for one-cell organisms and sea horses, the female of the species is the big Kahuna when it comes to incubating, birthing, and nurturing new young.

In late 1997, before I got pregnant, I went on a spiritual retreat. In the company of three laywomen and one kick-ass nun, I finally woke up to the female nature of divinity. And it changed my life for good.

Hidden behind God the Father, I found Sophia, which means "wisdom" in Greek, the female face of God. And anyone, male or female, who has ever encountered our ancient, primordial, and ever-present mother knows that, as the bridge between heaven and Earth, she has as much to do with creation as our universal father. Sophia is known by many names: Nature, the Queen of Heaven, the Blessed Mother, the Shekinah, the Holy Spirit, the World Soul. But she doesn't really care what you call her, because she is not some otherworldly egomaniac. All she really wants, like most mothers, is for her children to call her regularly, listen to what she has to say, and take her advice when she gives it.

I needed Sophia to prepare me for motherhood, which she lovingly did. My daughter was born less than a year after I first encountered the glorious Goddess within. I named her Sophia so that she'd always remember that she's not only the daughter of a powerful father but of a magnificent mother, too.

TAMI COYNE, 44, is a spiritually oriented career and life coach and the coauthor of *The Spiritual Chicks Question Everything: Learn to Risk, Release, and Soar.* She lives in New York with her husband and daughter.

Sophia

Sophia in Greek, *Hohkma* in Hebrew, *Sapientia* in Latin, all mean "wisdom." The Gnostic Christians believed Sophia was the mother of creation. Her symbol, the dove, represents spirit, and she is crowned by stars, a Middle Eastern icon, to indicate her absolute divinity.

Exploring Feminine Spirituality

The Feminine Face of God by Sherry R. Anderson and Patricia Hopkins

When God Was a Woman by Merlin Stone

The Chalice and the Blade: Our History, Our Future by Riane Eisler

The Myth of the Goddess by Anne Baring and Jules Cashford

Women in Praise of the Sacred by Jane Hirshfield

We'd Remember Women

I am woman protector of the universe
of all things ever created
nurtured by my own mother's milk
shoulders slightly worn but skin like silk
Back bent from carrying groceries and babies
and problems and issues and secrets and desires
and your stuff, his stuff and her stuff
Holding in passion
Holding in attitudes
Listening to opinions of moms and dads, husbands and children, aunts, uncles,
grandpas and grandmas, girlfriends, boyfriends, babies' daddies, ex-husbands, mr. right nows, mr. wanna be's, and mr. I only want to sleep with ya not be with ya
all with opinions to offer,
criticism to give,
but nobody's there at 2 in the morning to rock me to sleep, to wipe my tears, to listen to my dreams and desires and even my breath as I try to sleep yet again on a tear-stained pillow

I am woman
I walk and talk
my walk
We are women
We are grace and sensitivity and skill

I am Delilah who can whisper sweet nothings in your ear and can
make you say things you never thought that you would say
I am Hagar who can create life even when unexpected
and I am Sarah who can take it back
I am Bathsheba who was taken by the man but loved only one
I am Eve temptress personified
The diva of excuses
I am Mrs. Lot who learned that knowing all can preserve your body
but not your life
I am Deborah—prophetess, organizer, ruler of armies and PTA and
play dates and doctor appointments and your calendar and PG&E,
cable, and car bills and laundry and dinner and dishes and
homework and even when too tired making love at 12 midnight
because at least this way I can get you to put gas in the car or even
buy your own baby some diapers!!

Ruler of all things Deborah

I am Naomi, possessor of wisdom and patience that comes only
with age
I am Ruth, righteously giving homage to my elders

I am Rebekah and Dinah and Leah and Ataliyah and Filipah and
Bulhah and Rachael
All wrapped up into one

I am woman

Yolande Barial, 43, is the founder of Your Words Project in Oakland, California, empowering women of all ages to express themselves creatively by speaking their truths purposefully.

The Insight to Build Family

Section 2

Call it a clan, call it a network, call it a tribe, call it a family. Whatever you call it, whoever you are, you need one.

—Jane Howard, writer

Equality and Compassion Start with Our Families

KAREN BOURIS, author of *Just Kiss Me and Tell Me You Did the Laundry*

Toward the end of my daughter's first year of kindergarten, while my husband and I were driving, he brought up an idea he had for guaranteeing teachers affordable housing. A business and finance guy, he proposed a well-thought-out and innovative plan to house teachers that would have both community and federal support—and I listened, with eyebrow raised in disbelief, slight amusement, and a heart bursting with pride about how far we had come.

He would never have conceived of his grand "affordable housing for teachers" plan if he hadn't had everyday contact with my daughter's teachers and guessed that they struggled to make ends meet in Maui, where we live, where the cost of living is to the moon. He knew their names and some of their stories. He was in awe of their abilities, and in the fall, after the first month of school, he said, "This school is run by powerful female energy and nurturing. It's amazing!" I pointed out that most schools had mostly women teachers, women working in low-paying positions where housing was always an issue. (Even today, Elementary Education graduates are 89 percent women.) He had little awareness of these issues, and no amount of me yakking in his ear had the same impact as walking on campus, greeting and knowing teachers, feeling their power, and hearing children's joy.

And the reason he did drop my daughter off at school and attend many of the school functions was because I insisted, four years ago, that parenting, *as we knew it,* had to change. For the sake of our marriage, our kids, and (my grand plan) the world, we wanted it to be shared parenting, equal parenting, partnership parenting, whatever you want to call it. We—okay, it was really just me in the beginning—did not want a bitter marriage, with me the nag, mothering him and our children, and him emotionally checking out, self-medicating, missing the little penny candy experiences of our kids' lives. Tradition be damned, we wanted a new suit of clothes.

And the truth is, that until we can negotiate the terrain of our marriages and family life—until we can insist, demand, *simply ask!*—for what we need, we won't actively participate in ruling the world. We will be too busy balancing our lives and apologizing for it. Here's why sharing parenting will change the world: Yes, it allows women to have support in pursuing leadership positions in business and government and community, but it also allows men to come home, to know their children, their children's teachers, to learn firsthand about health care and waiting at the pediatrician's office for three hours, to feel torn over putting kids on antibiotics yet again, and to value housework as important work. Then they can, hand in hand with us, bring that knowledge and heartprint back out into the world.

Not all of us are from traditional families or couples—and you may, in fact, resent the hell out of the small screaming children or doe-eyed couple at the table next to you. But we all have family, whether it's cats and dogs or a built-over-time group of best friends who prop us up when we need it. We build families around us, whether we're single parents or single with parents we don't speak to, or a gay couple who has just adopted a precious child. And our family life, like Fifth Avenue minutes before the Macy's Thanksgiving Day Parade, is just waiting for the march of progress and activism to begin: to bring equality, respect, tolerance and acceptance, diversity, and compassion into our lives. This morning, start a revolution before pancakes.

KAREN BOURIS is the publisher at Inner Ocean Publishing and the author of *Just Kiss Me and Tell Me You Did the Laundry: A Couple's Guide to Negotiating Parenting Roles.*

We'd Pick Our Partners Wisely

It is the ability to choose which makes us human.

—Madeleine L'Engle, writer

The fact is, to my way of thinking, women do rule the world. We rule it a number of ways, partly by default, by our non-decision decisions, and certainly most directly by our very deliberate real-life choices, not only in how we live our adult lives but also by whom we choose to mate with. Because right in line behind our need to provide for our own physical and material well-being, to educate ourselves and find meaningful work, is one of our most critical adult tasks: how to choose a healthy life mate.

Let's imagine for a moment that we were all perfectly healthy and properly trained in this regard. For example, how different would our world be if we women had the raw self-love necessary to establish core conditions for relationships—nonnegotiable standards of eligibility for any man we might consider as a mate? What if we fell strictly for men who drew the line at all forms of violence and addiction, who made honesty a personal goal, and who wholeheartedly reserved their sacred sexual energy exclusively for us?

What if it were automatic and natural for us to lovingly insist that any partner of ours, be committed to a path of personal development? Be on the same page when it comes to doing whatever emotional healing and education are necessary to keep the symptoms of childhood traumas from corroding our shared adult lives?

What if we limited our selection of life partners to those who saw the wisdom of learning relationship skills? Who consider, as a matter of fact, the need to become emotionally literate and fluent in the language of the heart? Who would not argue with the importance of learning simple anger management and conflict resolution techniques?

For those of us who choose to create families, how different would our world be if we did not equivocate when it came to picking partners who grasped the supreme logic of parenting education *for both parents?*

How different would our world be if all women learned the critical adult task of enlightened and healthy partner picking? If we proudly declared, "For the sake of myself, my children, the community and the world, *I will not settle!*"

Let's imagine in our hearts and minds a world where women are really, really fussy. As my wonderful husband points out when we teach and counsel women (and men), "Women have more power and leverage than they use. Men want something women have got: themselves."

SEANA MCGEE is a psychotherapist and the author, with her husband, Maurice Taylor, of *The New Couple: Why the Old Rules Don't Work and What Does.*

~ Something to Think About ~

We Would Not Be Judged by Our Choices

Yes, I'm one of those. I have consciously chosen not to have kids. My husband and I have an extremely fulfilling life. We are focused on our careers, choosing professions that sustain and revive us. We have a dog, Maggie, whom we adore. We work hard and we play hard. We're active people—traveling, skiing, biking, and windsurfing.

I'm not a selfish person. I volunteer at our local community center; I have incredible friends, and I have wonderful relationships with my nieces and nephews. As I look at my life, I feel fulfilled and happy. So what is the problem?

Everyone else seems to have an issue with our choice not to have a family. "Oh," they say or, even worse, sidestep around the issue. My mother loves to slip in comments like, "But aren't you going to have a room in your house for a nursery?" I respond, "Do you really think I'm less of a woman because of my choice? Is my worth in your eyes tied to being a mother rather than friend, confidante, wife, sister, and daughter?"

If women ruled the world we would feel empowered to make the choice *not* to have kids and we'd never feel a twinge of guilt about it. We would never have to explain our reasons or feel as if we were being judged or letting other people down.

—Wendy Fist, 37

~

Families Would Be Based on Love and Commitment

It's so clear that you have to cherish everyone. I think that's what I get from these older black women, that every soul is to be cherished, that every flower is to bloom.

—Alice Walker, writer

Five years ago, at the age of 42, I traveled from my home in Brooklyn, New York, to Changsha, China, to adopt my daughter, Eleni. My bags were packed with diapers, baby clothes, formula, soft toys, and a tiny picture of a Chinese infant who was meant to be my daughter. As I left JFK International on that stifling August morning, I bid good-bye to my parents, telling them with an air of assurance that I'd be back in twelve days with their first and much-anticipated grandchild.

Looking back now, I realize that the months leading up to Eleni's adoption were among the most poignant and soul-wrenching of my life. Like many women my age, I had an irresistible emotional and biological urge to become a mother. But unlike others, I hadn't yet married, and at age 41, there were no real prospects in sight. Shortly after my 41st birthday, though, a friend and I had a long conversation, in which she encouraged me to follow my dreams. She told me of other women she knew, both single and married, who'd successfully adopted babies from abroad, and she suggested that I perhaps look into international adoption myself.

It seemed odd at first and more than a little sad to be abandoning the traditional path to motherhood, but my heart grew with the idea. I knew I wanted to be a mother, so I signed up with an agency, though at nearly every step of the way I was burdened with doubt as I questioned my ability to mother single-handedly.

What kept me going? The Chinese tell of an invisible red thread that connects each of us to the people in our lives we're meant to know. As I lay in bed on many a sleepless night, I gave weight to my practical, worldly concerns but ultimately succumbed to my heart's desire and to the power of the invisible thread that led me toward China.

On August 16, 1999, Eleni was given to me as my daughter. She was 8½ months old, curious, anxious, and about to become ill with a virus that lingered for weeks. In hotel rooms in China and all the way home, I nursed her back to health, and each day she grew a little stronger. During that time, Eleni learned to trust and depend on me, and I discovered that if I reached down deep I could find a well of strength, resolve, and tremendous love that would sustain us both, even in our darkest hours.

These days, Eleni is 5½ and happily living in Brooklyn. She loves SpongeBob SquarePants and Barbie, Rapunzel, and Shrek (as well as dim sum and the Monkey King), and she has adapted well to her home here in America. She has firmly seized me as her mom, staking claim with a fierce devotion. Yet there are times when Eleni asks about her birth parents in China, wondering whether they think of or miss her, and sometimes she simply grows sad. When she does, I try to remind her that a mother's love is eternal, granting her an indelible spot in her birth mom's heart. And I tell her that the red thread that brought me to Eleni encircles us all, transcending time and distance and transforming us into a family for whom race and culture know no boundaries.

If women ruled the world, I think we'd all feel more empowered to become mothers and create our own families according to our own inner searching and life plan rather than the belief that the traditional family, with a mother, father, and children, is the only acceptable path.

LAURA BROADWELL writes frequently about health and family issues for a variety of national publications. She lives with her daughter in Brooklyn, New York.

~ *Something to Think About* ~

THE DEFINITION OF *Family*

In February 2004, my best friend and her partner were married at City Hall in San Francisco. In a celebration that followed, tears stained my face as I watched them embrace their daughter, finally a recognized family. For 20 years they'd lived as a family—supporting each other, attending school events, eating meals together, crying, laughing, and loving each other. But they had few legal rights to protect and care for their family and each other. I walked that day among the protesters, looking at their angry, scared faces, and I wondered why it was so important to them that my friends not be married. How unfair it seemed that one person's love was legal while another's was labeled evil. I'd spent many weekends with my friends and their daughter. Never did I witness a fight or any feeling of resentment or conflict. There was a moment during that day when I had a vision of a different world, one where love and commitment defined a family—not sexual preference or marital status.

—Stephanie Peters, 34

The Lessons That Children Have to Teach Would Be Valued by All

If you only have one smile in you, give it to the people you love. Don't be surly at home, then go out in the street and start grinning "Good morning" at total strangers.

—Maya Angelou, writer

If women ruled the world, we would honor and hold sacred the time we spend with children. Children are our greatest teachers, but in order to really learn from them, we need to spend quality *and* quantity time simply being in their presence. I have a nursing degree and a graduate education. My husband of 35 years, Barry, is an M.D. and psychiatrist. We both were in school for a long time, and yet the education that we value the most has come from the triumph, joys, and struggles of our own relationship and from raising our three children. The experience of living in this family unit has taught us the most important lessons about life, spirituality, and opening our hearts.

There is a touching story about a little girl who would sneak into her newborn sister's room each evening after her mother put her to sleep. Her mother started observing her behavior and finally asked her what she was doing. Her reply was, "I think I'm forgetting what it's like in heaven. I'm asking her to help me remember." This is the greatest gift that children can give us. Just by being in their presence, we are allowed to remember our heavenly condition. Holding your baby to your chest allows your consciousness to expand, helping you realize that there is more to life than the daily "to do" lists and responsibilities that we get caught up in doing. If we're willing to watch and imitate our children, they can help us to remember the importance of just being.

Children repeatedly teach us about the wonder and magic of life. Anyone who has ever taken a small child on a hike through the woods knows about this sense of wonder. A child will look at everything, from the stones, leaves, sticks, ant hills, insects, to the dirt itself. While we as adults are busy rushing from point A to point B, a small child is catching all the magic in between. If we can slow our pace to match our children's, a whole new world will open up.

Children also teach us about unconditional love. There is nothing more precious than seeing your six-month-old baby gaze into your eyes and feeling her pat you tenderly with one hand while you nurse her. For that moment, nothing else exists except the pure love that she feels for you, her mother. If we can quiet our minds and really open up to receive the love, in all of the ways our children offer it, our lives would be changed.

In family we learn about peace, forgiveness, innocence, creativity, laughter, joy, enthusiasm, and many other noble qualities. Within this small home community, we learn how to live in the community of the larger world. If women ruled the world, there would be more honor and support given to the family system. We'd look at children as models of love in our lives, as our greatest teachers of many life lessons. Instead of busying ourselves with tasks that make no difference at all in the outcome of a family's life, we'd make our children a priority.

JOYCE VISSELL, R.N., M.S., is coauthor of *The Shared Heart, Models of Love, The Heart's Wisdom,* and *Meant to Be.*

"Time-Out" Would Apply to Grown-Ups, Too

No matter how old a mother is, she watches her middle-aged children for signs of improvement.

—Florida Scott-Maxwell, writer

My media scan has been looking the same for too long now: news about more bombs to drop, more corporate earnings to misrepresent, more laws to rewrite so we won't have to take responsibility for whatever unethical practice will help us get ahead. It makes me wonder, "Where are these people's mothers?"

I can't help it. I'm certain that we'd see far fewer press conferences with a corporate spokesperson or government appointee spinning a whole new brand of "truth" if their mothers were standing just off camera, arms folded and eyes fixed. I'm sorry, but you just can't pull executive privilege on your mom!

Now, I imagine that there would still be blood-thirsty dictators who'd have their moms taken out before they could get cornered in the kitchen at the next family gathering, but if women ruled the world, we wouldn't be unraveling our collective integrity faster than a ball of yarn going down the basement stairs. The politicians and CEOs would be answerable to their mothers first—with voters and stockholders watching closely for the response.

CEO: "Aw come on . . . all the other CEOs are setting up off-shore holding companies. It's not like it's illegal." CEO's mom: And if all the other CEOs were jumping off a cliff, I suppose you would, too. That's not illegal either—it's just stupid."

Administration official: "Hey, I was sure they were buying yellow cakes. I even have this letter that proves it." "Did you skip school the day they taught intelligence reporting? Even I can tell this is a fake."

Senator: "You just don't want me to have any friends in the Senate." Senator's mom: "I wasn't born yesterday. You call the EPA this instant, tell them you're sorry and you'll change that vote first thing tomorrow morning."

CIA operative: "I had nothing to do with that political coup! I was in my office all day and nowhere near that country." CIA operative's mom: "I've been able to tell when you're lying since you were 2 years old. Now go sit in time-out until you're ready to tell me what really happened."

War and Children

According to the Women's Learning Partnership (www.learningpartnership.org), in the past 10 years alone, wars have killed two million children, left 12 million children homeless, and more than one million have been orphaned or separated from their parents.

Really, when you think about it, elected officials and corporate executives are just hired help. And political office is a temp job at that. A good council of mothers—and mother equivalents—would be able to strip away the bureaucratic insulation and call these folks to task. No "staff" to take the blame. It's just doing chores on a bigger scale, and most moms won't put up with a half-baked job.

I'm certain that if the mothers of two countries went into a room to settle a dispute, they would not come out with the decision to send their sons and daughters out the next morning to kill each other. There would be a much different decision.

We may be a long way from having women rule the world, but we could start with a little more attention from the mothers. "Hello, caller number ten, you're on the air." "This is your mother speaking. Quit telling lies on the radio and get yourself home. You're in big trouble, Mister Smarty-Pants.'

LISA GRAHAM-PETERSON, 48, is a communications professional and single parent for two young men, ages 15 and 19. She remains amazed that her 5 foot frame still reigns supreme over her two towering teens.

We'd Create Family Within Our Communities

What families have in common the world around is that they are the place where people learn who they are and how to be that way.

—Jean Illsely Clarke, writer

Growing up number 10 in a large Catholic family of 12 in Chicago was an experience I'd never trade. Back then it was ordinary to see large families—most living on the same block or in the same neighborhood, all attending the same school together. There were families with nine, 10, and 16 children living in my neighborhood in the 1960s. We had what is rarely seen today—family raising family.

There was no day care then—not for any of us. Our world was a world where grandparents, aunts, and uncles looked out for us and took care of us while one of our parents worked a day shift and the other a night shift. They helped teach us how to tie shoes, read and write, and how to cook and clean. They spent countless hours teaching us crocheting and knitting, doing scrapbooks, putting together puzzles, making sure we went to piano lessons, and teaching us the importance of helping each other out. Together with our parents, they taught us respect, humor, manners, and the value of hard work and ethics. They showed us that adversity builds faith, faith builds strength, and strength builds character.

Generations Living Together

According to the 2000 census, nearly four million (3.9 million) American households consist of three or more generations living together; the figure has grown by 60 percent compared with a decade before. This trend is expected to increase due to adults living longer, the high cost of living, and an increasing number of grandparents and other relatives raising children.

My mother had tuberculosis before I was born and had to spend time in a sanitarium. She stayed there nine or 10 months, and it fell upon my father and other siblings, along with my extended family and community, to take care of everyone until she was healed. Many years later my mother survived cancer—three times. When my grandmother fell at age ninety and couldn't live alone anymore, my parents again opened their home and hearts and welcomed my grandmother to live with them. My sister moved back in with my parents and now helps out. You see, we remember. We know we were all blessed. We got it: Family takes care of family.

The way our communities are set up these days, each family is left alone to fend for itself—there is nobody to fall back on if you need a little help or someone is sick. Everyone lives in different parts of the states; we are too busy, so grandparents are put into homes and children sent to day camps while moms and dads are stressed and overwhelmed. If women ruled the world, we'd bring back the extended family, or if family wasn't available, we'd set up our communities in a more integrated, extended family sort of way.

LAURIE E. M. BRADLEY, 43, is a financial planner and outsource consultant and a freelance writer residing in Encinitas, San Diego County, California, with her husband and two sons.

Women's Work Would Not Be Defined as Housework

At the worst, a house unkept cannot be so distressing as a life unlived.

—Rose Macaulay, writer

If women ruled the world, our ability to keep a house would not determine our worth as women. Corporations hawking cleaning products would not automatically fill their advertisements with women who, smiling wistfully, scrub food particles off of countertops. If women ruled the world, we would never hear the phrase "Mama's got the magic of Clorox bleach" ever again. The use of bleach would not be considered some magical feminine mystery. Everyone would use bleach, and nobody would care.

We get the message from every direction, from our grandmothers to the media and many places in between. Housework is still widely considered women's work. Even in households where both partners consider things equal. Men who do the laundry or look after their children are applauded, while the women who do the same things seldom receive the same fanfare. It's expected of us, as women, to take care of the home, and if we happen to find a partner who helps, we are thought of as fortunate indeed.

On her wedding day, my mother-in-law received a set of dishtowels. Seven of them, to be exact, each depicting a woman performing a domestic duty. According to the towels, Monday is for laundry, and Thursday is for dusting. I don't know what the rest of the week entailed, because the rest of the set has long since vanished, although, through some strange twist of fate, I've inherited Monday and Thursday. I wonder if these towels, so popular in their time, somehow affected the collective consciousness of women. I consider the idea that perhaps women actually followed the schedule appointed by their dishtowels, but I quickly push the idea from my head. It's simply inconceivable to me. If women ran the world, our towels wouldn't mean a thing to us. Our seven-day schedule would read, "Dream, Enjoy Life, Explore, Create Change, Make Love, Think, Love Yourself," and that would just be the beginning.

Who Does the Housework?

A recent survey by United Press International of 2,177 women and 826 men found that women still do 76 percent of the laundry, 76 percent of ironing, 71 percent of routine cleaning, 67 percent of the cooking, 58 percent of the carpooling of children, and 58 percent of the grocery shopping.

LISA KILMER, 28, writer/mama who would much rather have a full life than a clean house. She lives in Kansas with her children, Brayden and Amelia, and her husband, Brian.

We Would Set Our Own Expectations for Our Lives

Although the world is full of suffering, it is full also of the overcoming of it.

—Helen Keller, activist, educator, and writer

In the spring of 1990, I received the most horrific news in my life. I'm still haunted by my father's heartbroken voice on the phone when he told me that my 23-year-old younger sister had killed herself. She had taken one of his guns, left the house, drove to a secluded parking lot, and shot herself in the head.

Everyone who knew my sister, Martha, was in complete shock. She always seemed happy and carefree. There were no warning signs. No previous attempts. No calls for help. I thought I was close to Martha. I thought I knew who she was. I had no explanation—only questions.

Technically, she didn't leave a note, but we found something she had written that was torn to pieces and left in her bedroom garbage can. It was a pouring-out of emotions from a person who spent her life trying not to let her family down.

Here is an excerpt from her letter:

> I wish my life would change. My mask allows no one to know how I really feel and the problems that I am experiencing, for I would never dare tell anyone. I've made all the wrong decisions. Some I regret. Some I don't. However, the ones I regret would be the ones that my family would never understand.

If women ruled the world, no woman would ever have to live in fear of letting people down, or not living up to expectations. She would stand confident in her own power and feel free to ask for help when she needed it without judgment or condemnation from any person or establishment. She would know how precious, relevant, and important every life is, especially her own.

Debbie Gisonni, 42, is the author of *Vita's Will, Snap Out of It: 25 Choices to Be Happy,* and the column "Be Happy." Her articles have appeared in the *San Francisco Chronicle, Simplycity, Living in Balance, Nonprofit World,* and more.

We'd Have a Room of Our Own

I have at last got the little room I have wanted so long,
and am very happy about it. It does me good to be alone.

—Louisa May Alcott, writer

One of the things I remember most about the opulent mansions (or "summer cottages," as Mrs. Vanderbilt and Mrs. Rockefeller referred to them) of Newport, Rhode Island, was the fact that the lord and lady of the house always had separate rooms. Imagine: separate bedrooms, space to relax and unwind without fear of intrusion.

I can only dream about the peace I would feel knowing that I had a safe, comfortable haven to slip off to when needed. A place where I didn't have to fight over closet space, drawer space, what size TV we had to have in the bedroom—and don't even get me started on the bathroom. In your own bedroom you wouldn't have to approve decorating ideas or bedding choice with anyone but yourself. You could display your collection of Asian artifacts right next to your scented candles, across from your bookshelf containing all your favorite old friends—nary a plastic toy, stray sports page, auto magazine, or Star Wars figure in sight (unless you wanted them).

I remember how much I loved my room growing up. From my tulip wallpaper and Barbie-filled room when I was 7, to my cool postcard collection, animation festival flyers, and art-adorned walls in high school, I reveled in being able to sit on my bed, listen to the music I loved, and shut out the world. Who didn't?

If I could create my own utopia, how perfect would it be to have a childproof door on this room of mine? "Mommy's playing in her room; she'll be out later. . . ." Of course, that part may be harder to realize without lots of outside help. I honestly can't imagine sleeping through the night *not* awakened by snoring or a child stepping on my head, so yes, utopia is a perfect description of this space.

I know I have a mini-meltdown pretty much once every few months. The day-to-day grind of constantly listening, caring for, being groped and pulled in every direction takes its toll. The way I cope is to shut down and find some "me time" (which in my case consists of an iced coffee and a long drive). Unfortunately, when I return home, that need for me time is not always satisfied. Some women practice yoga or meditation to find their center and escape from the fast-paced life we all lead. Others go to a spa or a girl's night out, or join a book club to allow themselves space to "breathe." Is this an adequate substitute for having our own room? I'm not so sure. There's a difference between allowing ourselves to indulge ourselves for a few hours and knowing we have our own permanent space for refuge on a daily basis.

Of course we do need companionship and intimate time with our partners, but maybe having separate rooms would even enhance this: "Your place or mine" could take on a whole exciting new twist. We deserve the space, the independence, and the freedom to express ourselves, be ourselves, and to be alone when we choose. Mrs. Vanderbilt was certainly on the right track; she knew that if Mama's happy, everybody's gonna be happy. . . . That said, where can I sign up for my own room, please?

Orlando resident SUZANNAH MITCHELL DIMARZIO, 30, is a wife and mother to Christian, 5, and Sophia, 4. She writes zines and aspires to publish books someday . . . and to finally get her own room.

~ *Something to Think About* ~

A Place to Hear Our Own Voice

After two weeks of bronchitis, a bout of stomach flu, and an incident involving my twin toddlers, a tub of Vaseline, and a desire to play beauty shop, I began to dream about isolation, to think that maybe Virginia Woolf had the right idea after all. In many women's homes if they're anything like mine, our notebooks are buried or finger-painted, and our thoughts and disrupted by telephones and boiling pots and voices clamoring for us, for what only we can do and be. In every aspect of our lives, we are expected to be present and engaged and persistent, without thought to reward or even just compensation. Where in any of this is there space and time for us? For reflection, meditation, peace? Every woman would benefit from a place to call her own, the only space in the world that asks nothing of her but simply to be, a place where she can close the door and let the world run itself for a change, and finally have the quiet she needs to hear her own voice and begin to listen.

—Jackie Regales, 25

We'd Speak the Truth Even in Difficult Situations

Half the misery in the world comes of want of courage to speak and hear the truth plainly.

—Harriet Beecher Stowe, novelist and abolitionist

I live in the Andean mountains of Peru, where I'm learning the art of healing from a remarkable Inka master. One day I was visiting my friend Ana Maria in Lima when Brother Thomas stopped by. Thomas is nearly blind but has a clear inner vision. He was on his way to visit a 26-year-old in the hospital who was very sick with bone cancer. A little while later, a big, burly, handsome man arrived. Francisco sat down to join us at the table in the garden and asked Ana Maria for a drink—"something alcoholic." I watched him talking jovially without understanding much of what he was saying or who he was, but then it occurred to me that he might be the father of Paco, the young man who was so sick.

I used the symbols we had been given in our Inka healing initiation to open my inner knowing and felt a growing compassion for the man. I said to Francisco (with Ana Maria translating), "It's important for you to talk to your other sons about what is happening to Paco, especially to the younger one."

He looked directly at me and said his younger son wouldn't speak about what was happening to his brother. "I am afraid to tell him. He is

"The biggest gift you can give your son is to speak with him openly," I responded. "First speak with Paco, then speak with Alvero, and then Alvero and Paco will be able to speak because they also have some things they need to say to each other. Do this soon, because Paco doesn't have much more time." It was almost as if I were channeling this information from a higher source.

"If I do this, will he get better?"

I sighed. "No," I said as gently as I could, because I felt that death was close by. "This is an opportunity for you. It will free Paco to die peacefully. You have a gift to give Paco, and he has a gift to give you."

Finally he stood up to leave and gave me a big hug. I could feel his sorrow and his fear like a dense black ball in his chest.

One day about three weeks later, I heard that Paco had died, and I found out through Ana Maria that Francisco had not spoken to his sons. If women ruled the world, speaking the truth in difficult situations would be integrated into our social structure. Women have been taught that expressing difficult emotions is acceptable; men haven't been given the same teaching or opportunities, and instead, in many cases, men are labeled as too emotional. Emotional vulnerability in men is not seen for what it is—a rich, deep sign of strength. Both men and women feel the same emotions; we grieve, cry, and feel anger, jealousy, and love. Giving both men and women the opportunity, skills, and confidence to speak the truth even in very difficult or angry situations is a necessary step in healing the communication gap among men, women, and families.

DIANE DUNN, 51, is an ordained minister from New York City and coauthor of *Gateway: Spiritual Journey on the Andean Path.* She lives in Cusco.

Our Relationships with our Mothers-in-Law Would Be Easier

Never rely on the glory of the morning
or the smiles from your Mother-in-Law.

—Japanese proverb

The moment I was knocked off the daughter-in-law pedestal came before I even had the ring on my finger. My husband-to-be and I were planning the wedding. We wanted something small and intimate, both meaningful and a rockin' good time.

I was really, truly, on my way to becoming the darling of daughters-in-law. But then I did something horrible: I thought the wedding was for my husband and me to celebrate our love and commitment. Not so, explained my mother-in-law, tenderly telling me about the true reasons for marriage, as if discussing the wedding night. It was about registering for china and silver (okay, it's true, I kind of adore the three place settings I got—enough for a family of, well, three!). It was about the flowers. It was about the number of wedding showers you had and who attended. And above all, it was an opportunity for the groom's parents to invite 120 of their most special friends to our party. Who knew? Arguments, loud and louder, ensued.

My mother-in-law and I settled our differences, and about eighteen months later we were close friends again. She was, and still is, one of my biggest cheerleaders and confidantes—even when I'm knocked off the pedestal and lying in a heap on the floor. But then I had a baby. Oh my

God! I'll say it again: Who knew? Who knew that she would tell me how to feed, bathe, rock, dress for success, comfort, and raise my children every moment she was in our presence? Who knew she would insist on giving my toddler children sugar at every turn, and tell me that if I didn't concede I was frighteningly mean? Who knew that after we firmly requested she not give our 4-year-old any more PowerPuff Girls paraphernalia that she would show up at our house with a PP scooter, PP townhouse, and four new PowerPuff girls to add to her massive collection? After a little therapy and the realization that this may be great material for a sitcom one day, I have realized that she loves us in the best way she can. All of her nutty behavior comes from a place of wanting to give her children and grandchildren everything. And I suspect that her desire to control and manipulate our lives—the classic mother-in-law archetypal behavior—comes from a feeling of powerlessness. Is this why my friends and I all share similar mother-in-law stories?

If women ruled the world, we would feel empowered in our everyday lives. We would know we could influence the world around us, we would deeply embody our own personal strength, and we would feel loosely in control of our own lives. Then we wouldn't bother with micromanaging the minutiae, picking on how someone folded a napkin incorrectly, or the fact that she didn't write a thank you note immediately, or all the petty things that we can do to each other (and to our partners, too). We could focus on what really mattered: loving each other, having compassion for all people, and being a responsible member of our communities.

Kathleen Simon, 46, is raising three healthy, happy children with her husband and the loving support of her in-laws. She lives and works in Austin, Texas.

Soccer Mom

Six A.M. Saturday. The big day.
Cut up oranges? Check. Dry clothes?
Soccer shoes? Water bottles? Coffee?

Beneath a cloud of down,
My 13-year-old and her flame-haired friend
Fall back to dreaming.

Early morning sky lightens.
Dawn. Show time.

Here, in California, countless miles from
Wars that never cease
I breathe morning air,
Whisper a peace prayer.

Keep the children safe
Save the mothers
Stop the killing
End the war

Here, in California under a pale blue late-fall sky
A determined team of pony-tailed girls
Give it their all.

When these girls rule the world,
Passion will ignite the Senate floor.
They won't be afraid of a fair fight,
And cannot help but remember today,
When they came from behind
And had to stand their ground.

When these girls rule the world,
Judgment will take a back seat as they shout:
"Freedom!" and "Justice!"

I cheer each goal from the sidelines,
Dispense cups of hot chocolate, peel off layers.
Grateful. For the joyous shouts of children,
For the dewy field,
For the valley,
For being a soccer mom.

JOAN GELFAND's books include *Music/Dream Series*, a poetry collection, and *Voice Over*, a novel. Joan received her M.F.A. from Mills College in Oakland, California.

We Would Cherish the Old as Well as the Young

Such to me is the new image of aging:
growth in self and service for all mankind.

—Ethel Percy Andrus, social activist

My grandmother is 97 and still lives in the home that was given to her as a wedding present. Nobody has the heart to move her into an elder-care facility, even though the cost of live-in care is prohibitive. She's so used to being independent and having all of her treasures around her. We've also toured quite a few facilities, and to tell you the truth, unless you have a ton of money to afford a country club–like setting, your loved one is stuck in an old building with bad food and ailing residents. So we do the best we can. We have someone who comes in every day, but at night she's all alone.

I'm the only daughter in our family, so I worry about what options there will be for my parents. Since women are seen as the traditional caregivers, taking care of my parents when the time comes will probably fall on my shoulders. I already have a good friend who is caring for her sick mother and her 3-year-old; she tries to see the humor in it as she diapers them both at the same time. But she also works full time, so the stress of managing her job, home, child, and mother is overwhelming.

I often wonder about the solution. If women ruled the world, would we value family more, would we direct government funds toward creating excellent elder-care facilities so the elderly wouldn't feel like they were being pushed out of their lives the second they needed a walker? I think we would, especially since the responsibility of aging parents often falls to us. Imagine if there were a system in place that allowed every person, rich or poor, a place to live in her or his old age. Nobody would have to worry about ending up homeless, or bankrupting family members to fund a caretaker, or being mistreated or fed disgusting food. Every room would have a window that allowed sunlight in; there would be activities and exercise and perhaps opportunities within the community where all the years of stored-up wisdom could be shared.

There could also be another option: that of taking aging parents into one's home. If women ruled the world, there would be some kind of compensation paid to offset the loss of work required by the adult who stayed home. Businesses would allow paid time off for elder care, just as they do in many countries for child care.

A society that cares for the elderly sets an example and lives by the belief that all people have something to offer their families, communities, and the world. It's time we start to link what many call the "breakdown of the family" to the lack of government support, funding, or programs that help those who are working so hard to keep families together.

Joyce Davidson, 48, is the mother of three children. She has plans to add on to her home so she can care for her parents when they need her help.

Stay-at-Home Fathers Would Be Commonplace

An atmosphere of trust, love, and humor can
nourish tremendous human capacity.
One key is authenticity: parents acting as people, not as roles.

—Marilyn Ferguson, writer and social philosopher

My husband, Dwight, and I talked about switching roles early in our marriage, before we had children, because I was more career-oriented than he was, but we didn't have the courage to do this when our children were born in the late 1960s. Then the lab where he worked shut down. I was going crazy trying to work half time and take care of the children. Dwight said, "Why don't we try switching? If it doesn't work, we can always switch back." That made the change seem less monumental, and I said okay.

Our boys were 1 and 3 years old when he took over. We both loved it at first. I was delighted that the person caring for the boys truly loved them, and I relished having a full-time career again. He was happy to be his own boss, spend time with his boys, and choose his own schedule.

But over time, he had some of the problems that stay-at-home moms face: isolation, lack of adult stimulation, and lack of the esteem we get from being paid for our work. And he had other challenges, such as dealing with the suspicious glances from mothers at the playground and getting the cooperative nursery school to change the sign from "Mothers' Room" to "Parents' Room." It was so unusual in those days for a father to be the primary caregiver that Dwight was interviewed for articles in the *San Francisco Chronicle* and *Newsweek.*

How much it matters to one's self-esteem to earn money, [was a revelation to both of us]. When Dwight took a job rewiring a neighbor's house, I complained, "But I want you to work on our house."

"But they're paying me to do it," he answered.

"I'll pay you."

"It's not the same."

At nursery school one day, the teacher asked what the children wanted to be when they grew up. Our older son, age 4, said, "Some days I want to be a fireman, but some days I just want to be a regular dad who stays home and takes care of the kids." I love to think that the rest of the world will someday think that *is* a definition of a regular dad.

Stay-at-Home Dads

According to the U.S. Census Bureau, full-time stay-at-home fathers took care of 189,000 children in 2002, up by 18 percent since 1994. Of the 23 million married parents of children younger than age 15, about 22 percent of the moms were at home full time, while just 0.5 percent of the dads were.

If women ruled the world, we would encourage men to be househusbands and primary child caregivers. We would let go of control and allow them to parent in their own way. We would share the pressures of the breadwinner role and gently insist that our partners take on the joys and responsibilities of child rearing.

ZIPPORAH W. COLLINS, 64, is a freelance editor and book project manager in Berkeley, California. She and Dwight have been married for 42 years and now delight in their new granddaughter.

We Would Be Role Models for Our Daughters

One is not born, but rather becomes, a woman.

—Simone de Beauvoir, writer, philosopher, and activist

Nine days before Mother's Day 1993, my mom died of breast cancer. My mother—nicknamed Maude, because she reminded many of actress Bea Arthur's pre–*Golden Girls* hit sitcom character—advised beauticians on the latest hair-cutting techniques and plumbers on the proper fittings. She entered kitchens in restaurants to demonstrate before stunned chefs the correct way to flip omelets and rarely missed an opportunity to instruct nurses on a better method of drawing blood. And she would always practically crawl under her car to make sure the mechanics drained *all* the oil. My mother was an original.

She taught me tolerance for diversity. Maude enjoyed talking to anyone, regardless of gender, color, age, sexual orientation, or religion. Once, at a checkout line, she tried to fix up a young man with a friend's daughter. When he said, "Probably not, madam, I'm gay," my mother, undaunted, replied, "Gay, schmay, everyone needs someone. So how about meeting my neighbor Allen?"

Mom taught me freedom of expression. True, mealtimes at our house caused a rise in Maalox sales. Compared to silent supper gatherings at my friend's homes growing up, dinner at my house was a Senate floor debate! But we were all allowed our opinions.

Equally important, my mother taught me that gender should not be

Organizations for Young Women

- Girls, Incorporated develops research-based informal education programs that encourage girls to take risks and master physical, intellectual, and emotional challenges (www.girlsinc.org).
- Girl Scouts provides an accepting and nurturing environment to help girls build character and skills for success in the real world (www.girlscouts.org).
- *New Moon* magazine is an advertisement-free publication of girls' fiction, poetry, artwork, letters, science experiments, and cartoons (www.newmoon.org).
- Rock 'n' Roll Camp for Girls is a Portland, Oregon-based day camp where girls can learn the basics of creating and playing music, coupled with empowering workshops (www.girlsrockcamp.org).
- Camp Fire USA provides all-inclusive, coeducational programs, designed and implemented to reduce sex-role, racial, and cultural stereotypes and to foster positive intercultural relationships (www.campfire.org).

a barrier to anything we wanted to do. From her I learned to fix toilets, repair appliances, use a saw, maintain a home, raise a child alone, and run a company. She believed a society was only as strong as its weakest link. Volunteering, and helping others to become self-sufficient and critical thinkers, was mandatory. These are amazing qualities in a leader, every one of them taught to me by my mother. Today, I am the founder of the National Organization of Single Mothers, representing the largest family demographic, because my mother allowed me to grow into myself instead of her deciding who I should be. She lived her life conscious of the example she was setting—she would be proud.

ANDREA ENGBER is the founder of the The National Organization of Single Mothers; editor of Single Mother; columnist and author of several articles and books including *The Complete Single Mother*, and mom to 18 year old son, Spencer.

Motherhood

Scud this, you son of a Bush!
Mother Of All Bombs is nothing less than the Mother Of All Insanity!
Let the wars be fought by mothers!
A new era for humanity would dawn
wars for a just cause
wars never again based on fiction and forged documents
wars fought only when real diplomacy failed.
Mothers would never sacrifice their children for anything less than that
and war would have a face
a constant reminder of the price we pay.
There would never be the shrug-of-the-shoulder indifference when discussing the dead
our tears would flow
every life lost
would have a face
and a story to be told . . .
the mothers would want to know.

A writer of fantasy-adventure and political poetry, Audrey Hardy resides in St. Paul, Minnesota, with her teenaged son.

We Wouldn't Question Our Parenting Choices All the Time

One's philosophy is not best expressed in words.
It is expressed in the choices one makes.
And the choices we make are ultimately our responsibility.

—Eleanor Roosevelt, former first lady

Just the other day my 16-year-old daughter shared with me a discussion she had in her Social Justice class at school. The teacher asked the students to think about the one thing their parents did in raising them that they would like to carry on in their own families. Apparently the kids all needed some time to digest and think about this, because the teacher had to give more instruction. "What did your parents do right?"

The kids got it. Of course, as my daughter was telling me this, a tinge of fear rippled through my stomach as I thought of all the unconventional parenting choices I'd made—which had she chosen to tell her class?

"Remember the time you found cigarettes in my car?" she asked. "I told them about that.'

The experience she described was the first time I discovered that perhaps my daughter was doing something that I didn't agree with. But I remember that day clearly because I took the cigarettes into the house, sat on the couch, and thought for a long time about what to do. On some level I knew the responsible parenting thing to do would be to ground her, or at the very least tell her the medical facts and how disappointed I was that she was choosing to smoke.

But instead I listened to my intuition and did what *none* of the parenting books would recommend. I told her I found the cigarettes in her car, and then asked if she smoked. She said that they were a friend's, and that no, she didn't smoke. I went on anyway, not wanting to miss this opportunity to get my point across. This is what I said, and what she shared with her class that day:

> I trust you to make good decisions in your life. You are old enough to choose for yourself and to live with the consequences of those choices. If you want to smoke, that is totally up to you, but I want you to be proud of your choices, which means not sneaking around and doing them in secret. If you want to smoke or have sex or whatever else, be willing to stand by your choice and claim your right to your own life.

If women ruled the world, mothers would feel more confident to turn inward for answers. Our daughters would be raised to feel their own power instead of living their lives with rules that are set up based on a black-and-white value structure—if you do this, then this is the consequence. Women are incredibly creative problem solvers who would most likely deal with disciplining their children in a new way if we trusted ourselves more and felt we had the right to make these basic "ruling" decisions in our homes.

Samantha Howard, 47, is a graphic designer by trade and an honorary Ph.D. in motherhood (from life experience), who follows her intuition and, because of this developed skill, has raised three self-reliant children.

Call to Action

Use Intuition as Your Guide

When we connect with the natural self, beyond our fears and inner battles, we discover a different source of wisdom. This inner voice has many names: intuition, inner wisdom, the voice of God, spiritual guidance, a higher power, beginner's mind, natural knowing. We all have different ways of experiencing this.

Some people see pictures or images; some hear actual words or messages. Some get glimpses of possibilities. Here's an exercise to try:

- Each morning, take five minutes to sit quietly and reconnect with your natural self. Stay in that place alert and aware, and simply notice what thoughts arise. Write down three or four that catch your attention.
- Act on those thoughts during the day in some way.
- Check back in with yourself at bedtime. What did you notice? Was the wisdom that emerged useful?

—From *The Peace Book* by Louise Diamond (www.thepeacecompany.com)

Equal Parenting Would Be the Norm Instead of the Exception

Equality for women demands a change in the human psyche more profound than anything Marx dreamed of. It means valuing parenthood as much as we value banking.

—Polly Toynbee, activist

My husband and I both used to work a 40-hour week—except that he made more money than I did. Because his job was deemed more important, I believed I should do more of the housework. In fact, I ended up doing about 90 percent of the cooking, laundry, housekeeping, and child care, including scheduling the doctor's appointments—even though we both worked the same hours. While this was happening, I certainly felt resentful and angry, but I also wanted to make up for lost time with my kids and wanted to be Supermom when home. Quality parenting, though, isn't defined by folded laundry, and I found myself seething sometimes but also being afraid, since I wasn't the bigger wage earner. In the end, though, I accepted it.

But then we had a major shock. My husband lost his job—and I got an opportunity for a promotion at my work, which I took, because we suddenly were desperate for my income. The brunt of the shock, though, hit my husband hardest. At first, he almost believed that I should continue to manage the household *and* work. His day with the kids was done when I got home, only to find this scary scene: house a mess, no food in fridge, kids a wreck. We both realized that life couldn't go on this way, and slowly, slowly, things got better. It's almost as if I had to teach him: this is how you make a shopping list; this is how you fill out the forms and sign them up for T-ball three months early; this is how you have to feed them healthy food so they don't have a sugar high and a fit and are prepared for school. Thankfully, he was ready to learn (usually!). He is even beginning to enjoy some of the pieces of parenting and being home. It is summertime, and the kids and my husband go to the beach and the park and play outside. And he even learned how to turn a grocery-shopping trip into an adventure.

Fifteen years ago, when I graduated from college, all I heard was how women get to do it all, how important it was that I concentrate on a career, that I could indeed rise to the top in my chosen field *and* raise great kids. However, somewhere on this journey I lost myself, and I started to believe that my time and work life weren't important—that my husband's life and work mattered more. When I used to bring this up to my husband, he pointed out that he was the major breadwinner and needed more down time, and it was my role to care for our children. Now we're both singing a different song.

Five Reasons Why Equal Parenting Is Good for Us

1. The more equality we have in our marriages, the happier we are being married.
2. Equal parenting is a great message for children.
3. It helps us to meaningfully prioritize our lives.
4. It supports both parents in having a rich family life and a rewarding exterior life.
5. It's good for society.

—Adapted from *Just Kiss Me and Tell Me You Did the Laundry* by Karen Bouris

My problem was that I believed that I—and I alone—should be able to do it all. I *should* be able to get up and make the lunches, take the kids to school, go to work, grocery shop on the way home, do the homework, and still make love a few nights a week. I was overwhelmed and exhausted, bitter and resentful toward my husband for having a much easier life. But now I see that I was wrong, and I was striving for the unattainable (and undesirable!). Who wants to do it all, after all? I needed to "do it all" with my husband. I needed to formally include him in our family and house care; otherwise, we were headed for divorce.

If women ruled the world, there would be more equality in parenting, so that mothers could feel creative and refreshed in their lives instead of barely surviving each day. Fathers would have stronger bonds with their children and relish the opportunities to share parenting. Women would feel confident in negotiating, both at work and at home, a plan that takes their goals and dreams into consideration. And, of course, the amount of money one partner makes would be irrelevant when dividing household tasks!

As I say all this, I have to admit that I bought into this system. I'm the one who felt disappointed with myself when I couldn't do it all to perfection. I could have drawn the line and demanded this equal parenting structure—but I was afraid. Fortunately, a turn of events required that we change, and our household was shaken up into a new and better family based on teamwork, shared responsibility, and mutual goals.

JENNY WHITNEY, 32, is a public relations assistant, who is raising two toddlers and trying desperately to win the game of tug-of-war she's currently playing with her husband.

We Would Teach Our Children the Importance of Volunteering

The human contribution is the essential ingredient.
It is only in the giving of oneself to others that we truly live.

—Ethel Percy Andrus, social activist

Volunteering is not some feel-good act of noblesse oblige; it's an effective answer to the pervasive narcissism of our consumption-crazy culture. Modern America is plagued with disconnections—blacks from whites, rich from poor, and, perhaps most troubling, parents from children. One of the greatest ways to bridge these divides is to teach children from an early age the importance of making service an integral part of their lives.

Children brought up to feel that their lives have a larger purpose beyond themselves are more likely to keep their own troubles in perspective—and less likely to open fire on their classmates. It helps them see beyond the importance of being popular to the value of being useful. The goal is to let them know that not everyone in the world is rich, white, straight, and healthy. I don't think you can teach them that without showing it to them firsthand. When families gather around to decide what they're going to do this weekend—go to the mall? see a movie? hit the beach?—volunteering should be among the regular options.

And in these multitasking times, overworked parents should happily note that family volunteering allows them to kill two birds with one stone: serving their community while spending quality time with their kids. It's also a powerful way to bring another dimension to your relationship with your children. For my own kids, volunteering together has been a profound educational experience—they've absorbed lessons they could easily have rejected if I had just preached them.

We are all born with an instinct for altruism and giving, as surely as we are born with instincts for survival, sex, and power. But like muscles that need to be exercised, our children's generosity and compassion can only be developed through regular workouts. Think of family volunteering as aerobics for the soul.

As we drive fancier cars, live in bigger houses, and work longer hours to pay for them, we can't help but recognize that something is missing. Stephen Covey, the best-selling author of *The 7 Habits of Highly Effective People* and a family-volunteering champion, describes volunteering as a win-win-win situation: "Communities win as the recipients of the services that families give. Parents win because they have an organized, workable program for teaching values and bringing their families together. And our children win because they learn the values that are so hard to come by in today's world."

If families are the bricks that make up a strong community, then family volunteering might just be the mortar that holds the community together.

Arianna Huffington is a nationally syndicated columnist, author of 10 books including the recent best-selling *Fanatics & Fools: The Game Plan for Winning Back America,* and cohost of the NPR program "*Left, Right, and Center.*" She lives with her two daughters in southern California.

Call to Action

Volunteer with Your Children

Find an organization in your community where you and your family can volunteer. Visit Volunteer Match (www.volunteermatch.org) and the Network for Good (www.networkforgood.org).

~ Something to Think About ~

Men as Volunteers

In my son's class there is only one father who volunteers on a regular basis to help the kids with reading. Pretty much every mom has a scheduled hour each week, whether she works full time or not. I also volunteer at a children's hospital and an environmental clean-up group where I've seen very few, if any, men. Our communities need more men who are willing to volunteer their time to keep worthy causes going that improve our towns and help those in need. As I speak with girlfriends about the shortage of male volunteers, we've come to the conclusion that women are raised to respect the value of service to others, whereas men may not consider this their social responsibility. If women ruled the world, or at least shared leadership, the structure of home (more equality and shared parenting) and business (men and women being paid the same for the same job, both with time off for caring for children) would be turned on its head. Perhaps then the job of nurturing a community would fall equally to men.

—Stephie Taghizad, 39

Connecting in Our Communities

Community means that we have a place where we belong no matter who we are.

—Hillary Clinton

Section 3

Introduction

The Power of Women with Purpose

Dolores Huerta, activist, cofounder of the United Farm Workers of America

I had years of experience working on community service projects before I started out as a schoolteacher in a community of immigrant workers. But after a while I couldn't stand seeing kids come to class hungry and needing shoes. I thought I could do more for my community by organizing farm workers than by trying to teach their hungry children. This experience made me realize that I had the power to create change. I also felt the responsibility. I began to see that one way I could harness and use that power was to get together with other women within my community, share the issues that concerned us, and then take a more powerful stand.

As a group with a purpose we can do amazing things. Look at grassroots efforts like Take Back the Night—originally a candlelight vigil in one crime-infested neighborhood in London, it has now grown into an international rally and march, organized by individual communities to peacefully protest violence against women, children, and families. Then there is MADD (Mothers Against Drunk Driving), another successful group formed by women, which started small in one community. Organizations like Feminist Majority train women as leaders and support women running for office so that more women can be included in policy making at every level. The impact of women in leadership positions, giving voice to issues of concern to them, can be great, from national decisions all the way down to community boards. Without these kinds of groups, without this kind of effort made by women throughout history, we wouldn't have women in congress right now influencing decisions on child and health care.

In my fifty years as an activist, I have also seen the power women have to influence peaceful resolutions. Women and children on the front lines of strikes or protests, for example, goes a long way toward inhibiting any violence that might occur and challenges the men to find nonviolent solutions. Many times when I stood on a picket line and violence seemed to be the next step, I was able to defuse it by injecting my energy and direction into the situation. When you have women, who are generally less violent than men, in leadership positions, it defuses aggressive behavior—where men might want to engage, women generally offer a balance.

Perhaps this is because women think differently and approach situations from an entirely different perspective. We have more of a tendency to accommodate instead of confront, and we don't feel like our egos are damaged if we have to make a compromise. Cezar Chavez used to say that more women should hold negotiation positions. Women approach the process differently asking, "There's a job to be done, how are we going do it?" They don't care as much about who gets the credit or blame; instead they focus on the solution.

Those are some of the powerful ways we can enact change in our communities that are available for any of us to begin right now. But there are also things in our communities that haven't been established yet, which are reflected in the essays that follow. I believe that these things would already be in place if women did rule the world—but I also know that it is possible to work toward them, especially if we continue to vote more women into leadership positions. Women can be the catalysts for the kind of change we so desperately need to see in our communities and our world; we already have more power than we know.

DOLORES HUERTA, 74, is the cofounder and first vice president emeritus of the United Farm Workers of America. The matriarch of eleven children, fourteen grandchildren, and four great-grandchildren, Dolores has played a major role in the American civil rights movement.

We'd Take Time to "Clean House" in Our Selves, Our Homes, and Our Communities

Service to a just cause rewards the worker with more real happiness and satisfaction than any other venture in life.

—Carrie Chapman Catt, suffragist and journalist

I am a dreamer and have always been. When I was young, I would wish for peace with every birthday cake. I grew up in a typically dysfunctional family of the 1950s. After bashing through the '60s and '70s and emerging battered by a number of life-sobering experiences, I began earnestly investigating different spiritual practices.

A few years ago, talking with a friend about the overwhelming suffering in the world, the heinous activity of world governments, and the insidious "victim" mindset generated through media and various religious factions, I wondered, "How the hell am I, one small person, going to do anything significant? Especially now that I have already lived most of my life." My friend simply replied, "You want to clean up the world, Gretchen? Clean up your own house!"

Although this certainly stopped me in my tracks, I remember thinking, "Yeah, right. . . . I get the expansive possibilities of that thought, but how will that help *right now!?* Time is pressing, don't you know!"

It has been years since that conversation. And it seems to me that it is the pressing of time with which we wrestle today. And cleaning one's own house appears to require time we either feel we do not have or don't wish to spend cleaning. We hire someone to do it for us in order to "save time," or we begrudgingly do it ourselves when we can no longer stand the dirt, or we just don't do it at all.

Cleaning a house is a metaphor for cleaning the greater house we call Earth and the smaller house which is our self. Since that conversation, I have experienced a renaissance of heart regarding this notion of cleaning, beginning with my family and reaching out into my community. My family now eats healthy foods without preservatives, we take herbal rather than pharmaceutical remedies, we recycle everything we can, and we are friendly with our neighbors. We have a garden with flowers that are slowly making their way down the street (the neighbors ask for them when we are thinning and pruning). We endeavor to keep the yard free of trash, and in reply, the neighbors tend to pick up, too, and the children are less inclined to drop wrappers and toys on the sidewalk.

Neighborhood cleaning is an evolutionary process, beginning within the confines of one's own "house." And what transpires, once we start cleaning, is the undeniable reality that when one attends to one's immediate circumstance, the energy generated compels change outside of one's personal space. People love beauty. With attentive cleaning of our house, we not only create beauty, but more importantly, we inspire the respectful treatment and gracious appreciation of the people and natural environment surrounding us.

GRETCHEN TARGEE was born in the midwestern United States in 1952 to a schoolteacher and newspaper editor. She moved as an adult to upstate New York and lives there still with her husband and children.

CALL TO ACTION

Make Your World a Cleaner Place

Plan a way to help beautify your community. Invite your neighborhood or child's class or book group. Here are some ideas:

- Plant trees in the community (check out www.arborday.org for ideas).
- Call local government offices to find out about neighborhood beautification projects.
- Look into replanting native plants in public spaces or in your own neighborhood.
- Help reinvigorate local recycling projects, education, and enthusiasm.
- Lobby your local supermarkets to use recycled materials or paper products instead of plastics. See www.thepetitionsite.com to create your own petition.

~ Something to Think About ~

Celebrating Life Passages

When I read about tribes of people around the world living in community, I feel that in the United States we really miss out by not having more rituals, initiation ceremonies, and community celebrations in general. There is nothing in place, outside some specific religious traditions, that marks transition as a positive thing. Sure, we have birthdays, but a cake and balloons is a far cry from being draped in white and showered with flowers as the whole village celebrates your approaching womanhood. And what is there for women when they reach old age? We have nothing in place to celebrate the gifts of wisdom and life experience these women now offer the community. Instead, we drop them off at a rest home, assuming they are no longer of use to the community. If women ruled, I can't help but hope we'd look backward to ways of old that joined people together, in celebration and life-affirming community ritual.

—Olivia Piatek, 67

We'd Support Tolerance and Acceptance of All People

In the end, antiblack, antifemale, and all forms of discrimination are equivalent to the same thing—antihumanism.

—Shirley Chisholm, politician and educator

"I don't understand what you mean," said Audrey.

"Of course you do. We've been over and over this."

Audrey's eyebrows crinkled and she pursed her lips tight. She listened but kept washing the dishes. Randi saw this, stopped drying, and took a step back, still holding the towel in her left hand. Audrey quietly turned toward Randi.

"We go to the movies all the time. We visit friends, volunteer at Lavendar Books, and work in our garden. What else do they want us to do?" By now Audrey's face was completely flushed, her dark brown hands glistening with water.

"I know we do. That's not what I'm talking about. You know." Randi shuffled her feet and put the dish down she was drying. Then she just stood there in front of the kitchen window. Her blond hair looked almost white in the sunlight.

Audrey turned her eyes down. Her whole body became limp, and tears rolled down her cheeks. Randi put her arm next to Audrey's.

"It doesn't matter to me," Audrey said.

The sound of broken glass interrupted her. They both walked into the living room. Their bay window was shattered. Audrey stopped crying, put her dishcloth down, and crossed the shard-covered carpet toward the window. She picked up the brick and put it on the stack by the front door.

"Soon we'll have enough for a whole new wall," Randi said.

Interracial Marriage and the Constitution

In 1967, the Supreme Court ruled in *Loving v. Virginia* that a ban on interracial marriage was unconstitutional. The law was overturned in Virginia and 15 other states (14 had already repealed similar laws). Still, a dozen states kept the ban on interracial marriages on their books for years, though the laws were legally unenforceable. Alabama was the last state to repeal their unconstitutional ban on interracial marriage, in 1999.

Tolerance.org provides education and tools for teachers, parents, and children to promote antibias activism in every venue of American life.

Dixie Treichel, 48, is a Minneapolis artist consultant and multidisciplinary artist, humanitarian, and an advocate for civil rights and environmentally safe energy. Her philosophy is that by collaborating creatively, we can transform greed and indignation into cooperation and tolerance.

~ *Something to Think About* ~

A World Without Fear

If women ruled the world, I wouldn't be afraid. I'd be able to watch the news without being ill. I'd be able to look my father in the eye and tell him the truth about me. I wouldn't worry that my friends might not be able to marry. I wouldn't spend time thinking up escape plans to send people to Canada to avoid a draft. I wouldn't dread family gatherings where all the talk is of sports, cars, and the military. I could walk in my neighborhood at any hour, wearing whatever makes me happy, and be safe and comfortable. I wouldn't need to write under an alias or assume online personas. I could speak my heart without censure. I could fully and freely express myself without endangering my job. My true self would be accepted and would not have to hide.

—Catherine Fahey

We'd Communicate in a Relational Way

If we have no peace, it is because we have forgotten that we belong to each other.

—Mother Teresa

Words have power. Every novelist and essayist knows this. Poets recognize it. So how would a woman's way of communicating be different if our words were truly heard and reverenced? How do we instinctively use language?

Men tend to express themselves in a linear fashion: who, what, when, why, where—this is the architecture of a masculine mind. Our world today contains the living monuments of those male words within our politics, economics, power structures, and relationships.

Women instinctively seek relational words. We speak linearly, but we harbor an enormous possibility of words within us, a hidden vocabulary. If we begin to change the words we use, we can change the world.

Let me give a small example of translating a linear vocabulary into a relational one. When my husband and I ended our marriage, he verbally announced, in a linear way, that the money belonged to him. I realized instinctively that only one word needed to be changed. For three years, every time he said "my money" (which was often), I said "our money." That was it. I slowly tilled his linear vocabulary into a relational one. When we finalized our separation, the ledger had two equal sides.

Origins of Language Concepts

Country: From *contrata regio* (Medieval Latin), "region on the opposite side"

Home: From *ham* (Old English), "village"

Peace: From *pax* (Latin), "state of security obtained under Roman rule"

We must recover the words that create a more connected way of being and relating to one another. Here are a few examples. Women hold a very deep understanding of country within them—much different than the usual sense of geographic boundaries and ideologies. For women, the root word is *home*. Any woman from any culture can say the word *home* and know it is the ultimate country-of-the-heart. Love and tolerance grow in homes; war and division grow in countries. *Country*—with its linear history of protectionism and defense—actually destroys the root word *home.*

Sadly, the word *peace* has also begun to be used in a linear fashion. This is our most difficult word, the one that most needs our attention. *Peace* in a linear world means a political solution, often imposed. A woman knows the peace of holding a newborn child. Such a peace has no ideology. This is the peace women must rebirth, in word and heart, now. It is not peace if the Middle East is quiet. It is peace when a Palestinian woman, an Israeli father, and an Iraqi son behold the world they live in with the soundless wonder of contentment and joy. The true meaning of peace is: *We are all one.*

Lastly, the word *economy*—linked as it is to finance—impoverishes and ravages our soul. True economy comes when women teach their children they must "share." We know these root words in our heart, but we do not say them in a global context. Instead, we teach survival—how to survive in a linear world. But now, in order for the world to survive at all, we must reteach the root words.

If we speak of the sacredness of *home* and never again say *country*; if we say *we are all one* instead of *peace*; if *economy* becomes *we share*—then slowly, the axis of our linear world will sift from division to wonder.

BARBARA ERAKKO TAYLOR, a semi-hermitess, has authored two books on silence. Today she weaves prayer shawls.

We'd Dialogue More and Argue Less

We all know we are unique individuals,
but we tend to see others as representatives of groups.
—Deborah Tannen, writer

When September 11, 2001, happened, I was working for a Silicon Valley start-up that prided itself on its international flavor. Out of a total of 100 employees, 40 countries were represented. When I joined this company, I quickly noticed a smiling Egyptian man named Ayman, whose cubicle was near mine. While Ayman was a devout Muslim and I a churchgoing Christian, the beginning of our friendship found us discussing our religions, where we shared our common goals of helping the poor, being faithful to God, and showing kindness to others.

Ayman had been born and raised in Egypt. Unfortunately for Ayman, he was attending a technical conference in Germany when the terrorist attacks of September 11 took place. Because Ayman looks Middle Eastern, he spent three harrowing days in Frankfurt, Germany, trying to get back home. Later Ayman told me how strange it was during those three days when perfect strangers would call him bad names (in German), obviously judging him as evil simply because he looked Arabic. During these three days, Ayman's wife (who wears the traditional *hijab* head scarf) and three young children in California were afraid to go to the store for groceries, lest they be hassled or attacked by angry Americans about 9/11.

At the time, I was part of the adult education committee at our church. I felt a particular responsibility to get the word out that Islam was *not* about flying planes into buildings—but was as much about treating our fellow human beings with kindness as any other of the world's enduring religions. So I asked Ayman if he would be willing to help me organize a series of Sunday morning talks to our congregation about Islam.

During those seven Sundays, bridges were built and misunderstandings clarified as we learned what Islam was really about. In the end, I think our congregation learned more about Islam from meeting Muslims and getting to know them than they did from the material being taught. It is much more difficult to accept generalizations about an entire people (like Muslims) when you already have met several of them whom you know to be hard-working, decent, and ethical people. If women ruled the world, I believe we would dialogue more and argue less. We'd build these sort of nonconfrontational discussion groups into our community structures, so that instead of judging or being afraid of our diverse neighbors, we would build bridges of understanding.

Peaceful Tomorrows

Peaceful Tomorrows is an advocacy organization founded by family members of September 11th victims who have united to turn grief into action for peace, in part by providing an open dialogue on alternatives to war. The group has asked presidential candidates to refrain from using 9/11 imagery in their campaign ads and has joined vigils for the unseen casualties of the "war on terrorism" in Iraq and Guantanamo Cuba (www.peacefultomorrows.org).

Alexa Wegener, 44, is an engineer raising two boys with her husband, who is also an engineer. The entire family has enjoyed learning about Islam, attending a local mosque, and sharing cultural traditions with their new friends.

Call to Action

Start Talking and Expand Your World

We often find ourselves in groups that embody the "birds of a feather flock together" philosophy. Imagine how, in our homogenous groups—such as those that include church friends, work colleagues, or school friends—we can expand our understanding of the world. How can we learn about other cultural practices, religious traditions, and the issues that affect different socioeconomic groups, races, genders, and ethnicities? How can you begin a dialogue group in your community?

The Animosity Between Girls Would Disappear

Girls are often their own and other girls' worst enemies.

—Rosalind Wiseman, writer

I don't like to think that I foster any kind of revolting socially ingrained jealousy towards other women.

But.

It struck me today that there is a streak of it. It runs so deep in me that I don't even realize it's there. Until I start to think about why I'm standing in the bathroom at work seething with rage over an unspoken rivalry with a new girl I have absolutely nothing against.

Good Books about Girls

Read up on girl hate, competition, and adolescent life:

Queen Bees and Wannabes: Helping Your Daughter Survive Cliques, Gossip, Boyfriends, and Other Realities of Adolescence by Rosalind Wiseman

Odd Girl Out: The Hidden Culture of Aggression in Girls by Rachel Simmons

Girl Wars: 12 Strategies That Will End Female Bullying by Cheryl Dellasega and Charisse Nixon

Reviving Ophelia: Saving the Selves of Adolescent Girls by Mary Pipher

Ophelia Speaks: Adolescent Girls Write About Their Search for Self by Sara Shandler

Please Don't Kill the Freshman: A Memoir by Zoe Trope

School Girls: Young Women, Self-Esteem, and the Confidence Gap by Peggy Orenstein

I am standing there, mentally picking apart her features, her body shape, her conversations with the guys we work with. I am watching their interactions, and I am suddenly seeing her not as a coworker, not as another woman living in the same world that I am . . . but as *competition.*

This girl is certainly not a threat to my job. But it seems that suddenly she is a threat to my femininity.

I put on more lipstick.

It's important for us as women to question our socially ingrained responses. To wonder *why* we pit ourselves against other women, why other girls may feel like a threat.

Where did this insane cruelty toward each other come from?

The things I grew up with, the TV shows, *90210,* girls against girls, that slut, that whore. Cheap girls, girls who don't respect themselves, so screw it, I won't respect her either. Girls getting stepped on, girls getting trashed by their best friends. Girls getting left behind, screwed over for a guy who is never worth it. Right?

You know what I'm talking about. Have the words come out of your own mouth? I admit they've come out of mine. They came out of my mouth today. "I hate that bitch." We have to learn where it comes from. We have to keep from passing it onto our daughters.

I'm ready to look for the end.

If women ruled the world, there would be no need for women to be pitted against each other to gain some invisible ground we believe needs to be claimed just so we feel powerful. We'd learn from an early age the skill of supporting each other, rather than looking for and pointing out weaknesses in others in the hope that we can feel better about ourselves.

Mz B runs a feminist zine distribution called gluestick distro out of the San Francisco Bay Area. This piece previously appeared in her zine *the fog of clarity part 2.*

Personal Space Would Be Respected

There's a very good reason why women live longer than men. They deserve it.

—Estelle Ramey, endocrinologist

Okay, so sue me, I don't drive. Inconvenient as this peculiar affliction is at times, I'm here to tell you that lack of vehicular competence is not without its perks. I am not, after all, personally responsible for the depletion of the ozone layer, plus I am far less likely than my four-wheeled friends to commit inadvertent homicide while conducting witty badinage via cell, chugging a latte with all the trimmin's (Lunch! Who has time for lunch?), and piloting a 200-horsepower vehicle all at the same time.

Verdant homicide, however, is not out of the question. You see, we nondrivers rely heavily on the quaint institution of public transportation. (You know what I mean . . . buses, subways, that sort of thing.) And, therefore, we tend to encounter actual *members of the public*—some of whom are just too goddamn annoying to live. I call these guys the "space cases."

No, not "space" as in "Oh, man, I smoked so much weed a couple of decades ago that I can't remember my own name; can I have some of your money?" And not "space" in the ever-popular Peter Pan sense: "I'm sorry, Wendy, but you're going to have to cancel the caterers. . . . I just need, you know, my space." No, what I'm talking about is the guy who is so big and bulky, or whose ego is, that he couldn't *possibly* confine his hulking corpus, his bloated senses of self, to the so-called seat that he has shelled out the princely sum of, say, $1.50 to occupy. The guy who, in short (or in tall!), unquestioningly assumes his rightful place in the world—and yours, too.

Now, never mind that I pay the same fare as Mr. Space Case—there is, after all, no such thing as business class on public transportation. Never mind that at times in my life—that is, the hugely pregnant ones—my posterior has certainly out-spanned the lame asses of many of the fellows next to whom I have sat (or rather, huddled, squished into the corner, miserable and hating their space-hogging guts). A guy walks down the aisle, plops into the adjacent seat, and the next thing you know, his thigh is pressing against your thigh, his elbow is jabbing your ribs every time he flips a page of the sports section, and God forbid the public transportation unit should take a sharp corner, because this bruiser, muscle-bound as he is, just can't prevent his body from falling into yours.

In leaner times, I have actually conducted *en route* experiments just to make sure that my petite physique, those tantalizingly unoccupied inches of my seat, weren't serving as a subliminal invitation for invasion. I have purposefully positioned myself to occupy every last millimeter of my allotted area. Sat with my legs planted wide, even though I'm really more comfortable crossing them: *Catch a (nonverbal) clue, Buster; the boundary has been drawn.* And guess what? It didn't make a whit of difference. Large guys . . . lapped over and made body contact. Little guys . . . lapped over and made body contact. Guys with hip haircuts and laptops, guys with dreads and yoga mats, guys with filthy clothes and booze-hardened faces, guys with "Go Cal" T-shirts and textbooks under their arms . . . they all lapped over and made body contact.

Women don't do this. They just don't. And neither should men, if for no other reason than this: It makes women uncomfortable. That's why, if the fair (well, fairer, anyway) sex ran the world, these "space cases" would be plucked from their seats at the first sign of encroachment and whisked off to a place where their talents could be put to good use: the NASA training program. After all, there are no boundary issues in outer space.

AUTUMN STEPHENS, 47, is the author of the Wild Women series of biography and humor and the editor of *Roar Softly and Carry a Great Lipstick.* She lives in Berkeley with her nuclear family.

~

The Sexual Double Standard Would Disappear

Our society treats sex as sport, with its record breakers, its judges, its rules and its spectators.

—Susan Lydon, writer and political activist

The sexual double standard has long been used to keep women in their place. In biblical times, men could have more than one wife, but women could only have one husband. A man caught with a "prostitute" (and men had the power to define who was a prostitute) was seldom punished to the same degree as the woman, who was often stoned to death. Honor killings—the killing of a woman whose behavior "disgraces" a family—still occur in some Islamic countries today.

Historically, in the United States, a woman was identified as her husband's property and could be legally beaten with a stick as long as the stick was no wider than her husband's thumb. During the antebellum period, white male slave owners could have sexual relations with black female slaves while society turned a blind eye to the activity. Any form of protest on the part of the woman most often resulted in her death. Married men throughout history have had affairs and "kept" mistresses without society giving their behavior a second thought. (Remember President Kennedy's behavior and how the press ignored it?) However, if a woman behaved that way, she was demonized, considered a freak, and otherwise chastised by society.

Think about your high school days. Whether it was the 1950s, 1970s, or even today, boys who serial dated were "studs" or red-blooded American males and the envy of their male peers, while girls who serial dated were "sluts" and generally were not the envy of anyone.

The fuss over the Janet Jackson and Justin Timberlake Super Bowl fiasco in 2004 is yet another example. Why is Ms. Jackson subject to all the fallout? Mr. Timberlake performed the actual bodice ripping! Both apologized for the incident, but only Ms. Jackson was "uninvited" to the next awards show; only she was barred from making any contribution to *The Lena Horne Story;* only she her statute removed from Disneyland.

If women ruled, sex would no longer be used to prove one's position or power over someone. Sexuality would be seen as a normal of aspect life, meant to be enjoyed by all. Judgments that label sexual behavior as bad or good would be abolished—or at least doled out equally, no matter what gender, for the same behavior. Society would not expect women to be pure, while supporting men's pursuit of sexual experience.

A Historical Double Standard

Victoria Woodhull was the first woman to run for president of the United States, in 1872. She openly advocated free love and was demonized as "the prostitute who ran for president." She then caused a major sensation by exposing a secret marital affair of one of her main detractors: Henry Ward Beecher, a prominent New York preacher of Puritanism and sexual restraint.

LAURIE L. ADAMS, 45, is a homemaker who lives in McKean, Pennsylvania, with her husband. They have three children and two grandchildren. Laurie holds a B.A. with honors in History from Edinboro University of Pennsylvania.

Call to Action

Examine Your Own Attitude about Sexuality

- Do you have conflicting feelings around the concept of "good girl" versus "bad girl"?
- Are there any stereotypes you hold about motherhood and sexuality—are moms allowed to be sexy?
- Do you feel you need to express yourself sexually according to what's been portrayed in movies or other media?
- Do you feel understood when you express your sexual thoughts, concerns, ideas to your partner?

We'd Fund Programs That Support Family

Those whom we support hold us up in life.

—Marie Von Ebner-Eschenbach, novelist

As I drive around neighborhoods these days, I rarely see people outside on their front porches or in their driveways talking to their neighbors; we've all built such high fences we can barely see who lives next door. Then there are gates and security stations with guards who announce one's arrival—making sure the riffraff have no way of entering. We've fenced ourselves in to the point that our family units have become islands of isolation unto ourselves.

I remember moving to a new community after my divorce, not knowing a single person, and feeling very alone. When an old friend mentioned that I should try finding some other single moms with kids my kids' ages (I reported that I lived in a family neighborhood), I discovered that there were no single moms on my block. I asked at the kids' school, but the the school wasn't allowed to give out personal information.

Months later, on the bulletin board outside a grocery store, I saw a flyer on the bulletin board outside a grocery store for a single mom's group. I decided to go to the meeting and was shocked to find that there were three single moms within walking distance of our home. So all those months I spent feeling alone, trying to help my kids make friends and adjust to a new school and new neighborhood while going through the trauma of divorce were unnecessary: Support was there all along, safely trapped behind our fences—we just didn't know it.

If women ruled the world, we'd fund more programs that support family, such as child care or even in-home cleaning help, so mothers would have more time to nurture the family. Job sharing, part-time employment, telecommuting, flexible working hours, paid leave for child and elder care, and paid paternity leave would all be programs that would lighten a parent's load, lower stress, and most certainly increase productivity. We need more support groups (especially for single moms and abused women and children) that are part of every community, like a post office or drug store, so that no matter where a woman moved, she would have a place to check in and meet other women to receive the support she needed.

Amanda George, 30, is the mother of two children ages 3 and 7. She now runs a single mom group in her community and is thriving in her new post-divorce life.

Support for Single Moms

The Web site www.SingleMomsConnect.org is a nonprofit organization that brings single mothers together as support partners and friends. Moms create an online personal profile based on areas of interest, life experiences, number of children, stage of singleness, or other chosen criteria. A search by zip code gives moms access to other moms within their immediate area, which broadens support and community opportunities, including child care co-ops, co-housing options, and mentoring programs, as well as social outings, family potlucks, and holiday events.

Also try these sites:

- www.familysupportamerica.org strives to transform our society into caring communities of citizens that put children and families first and that ensure that all children and families get what they need to succeed.
- www.proudparenting.com serves as an online portal for gay, lesbian, bisexual, and transgender parents and their families worldwide.
- www.familypride.org, run by the Family Pride Coalition, aims to advance the well-being of lesbian, gay, bisexual, and transgendered parents and their families through mutual support, community collaboration, and public understanding.
- www.singleparentsnetwork.com offers a list of Web sites, articles, information and support boards for single parents.

~ Something to Think About ~

FEDERALLY FUNDED CHILD CARE CAN AND DOES WORK

The military has an excellent child-care system that could be used as a model for the rest of the country. In 1989, the Military Child Care Act (MCCA) was enacted by Congress. The goal of the act was to improve the quality, availability, and affordability of military child care. We need a similar act, with similar funding, to address the lack and expense of quality child care for ordinary citizens. Teachers in military day-care centers are well compensated and trained, with positions comparable to other jobs on base that require similar levels of training, education, and responsibility. The costs of these quality improvements were not shifted to parents, because the U.S. military subsidizes the cost of its child care. Military families pay on average 25 percent less for child care than do nonmilitary families. And 95 percent of all military child-care centers (compared with 8 percent of civilian child-care centers) meet the accreditation standards developed by the National Association for the Education of Young Children (NAEYC). Perhaps it's time that Congress holds corporations accountable to the same standard for their workers.

—Megan Cuddihy, 31

We'd Form a Society Based on Partnership

Snowflakes, leaves, humans, plants, raindrops, stars, molecules, microscopic entities all come in communities. The singular cannot in reality exist.

—Paula Gunn Allen, writer

The Mosuo people are an indigenous, non-Chinese ethnic minority who live in villages around Lugu Lake in Yunnan Province. They live in large matriarchal families and do not practice marriage as we know it. Instead, they practice "visiting marriage," a system whereby the man visits his lover at night and leaves before daybreak to return to his mother's household. Children born of their union are welcomed and cared for by the birth mother and her family, with never a worry about "legitimacy" or paternity. There is no moral judgment associated with sexuality.

At Lugu Lake, my guide and translator, Tami, took me into several Mosuo homes. At one of the homes we were greeted by the matriarch, her youngest sister, Gehtumah, and her daughter Yodji. We were invited into the hearth room to sit around the fire. As we talked, Yodji motioned to Tami to ask me if I had any children of my own. I said, "No."

"How is it that you are your age without any children?" Yodji inquired. The question hit me with an unexpected emotional wallop. I felt my eyes fill with tears.

"Are you all right?" Tami asked.

"Yes, I'm okay," I whispered, trying to choke back the emotion that overpowered me.

Tami asked me, "Did you want to have children?"

"It's complex," I replied, trembling. How could I explain my sorrow and how it rushed upon me just now like a powerful wave? How could I tell them that when a teenaged girl is unmarried and pregnant in my world she is scorned and ashamed that her offspring will be illegitimate? How can I explain illegitimacy to a people who know that every child born is precious and sacred and whole? How can I tell them that it felt like my baby was ripped from my womb—but at my own bidding—because I couldn't bear the shame?

My tears increased as these thoughts filled my mind. Yodji spoke, offering a solution. Tami translated. "You can have one of my daughters," she said.

Thinking she was joking, I tried to make light of it by saying that it would be hard to explain that to U.S. Customs. But Tami told me that Yodji was serious, that Mosuo people don't view children as belonging to one specific parent, but rather as a blessing to the whole family and whole community. Yodji had already given her oldest daughter to her sister who was childless. Giving another daughter to a childless American woman made sense to her.

"I would love to have your daughter," I said, with a better understanding. "But it is not possible."

Back at the hotel I spent a restless night. In the early hours I awoke with a profound sense that something had shifted inside. I realized I had carried the enormous weight of the guilt of my sexuality and abortion for

A Modern Matriacrchal Society

The Minangkabau, located in West Sumatra and populated by four million, are the largest and most stable matrilineal society in the world today. Their customs include matrilineal descent and women's ceremonial roles. Read about their culture in Peggy Sanday's book, *Women at the Center: Life in a Modern Matriarchy.*

more than 30 years. I was worn out. But in the presence of these gentle people, a new understanding came to light. It was not I who was guilty; it was the structure of the society in which I lived. My society said I was wrong, it attached morality to sexuality, and it made me ashamed of my body, my passion, my pleasure. In my world, I had felt compelled to eliminate the pregnancy because there was no infrastructure to support me. In my world, that was all the truth I knew.

At Lugu Lake I found a new truth. I found a society based on partnership rather than on dominance and ownership. I found a society without rape or domestic violence and where neither women nor children needed to be made "legitimate" by marriage. Instead, the Mosuo family infrastructure provides for every human being—from the time of birth until the time of death.

In the Mosuo villages I often heard the women singing. Sometimes they sang love songs and sometimes songs to their beloved Goddess, Gemu. Always their voices rang out clear, bright, and strong. *"Madami!"* they would sing, a word not easily translated into English, which means something close to "Wow! Awesome! Marvelous!"

Whenever I think of the Mosuo people and how they have preserved such a beautiful and peaceful culture, I think, yes, indeed, Madami!

Diane Wolverton is a writer and business educator. She recently released her first book, *Return of the Yin: A Tale of Peace and Hope for a Troubled World.*

We'd Make More Time to Play

Every friend represents a world in us, a world
possibly not born until they arrive,
and it is only by this meeting that a new world is born.

—Anaïs Nin, writer

I am a quilter, though not of the kind that probably comes to mind when you think of one: a gray-haired, grandma-type who wears a house dress, stockings rolled down around her ankles, and drinks decaf. When I tell people I quilt, they usually say, "My grandma/mom/aunt does that." I'm what you'd call a "young quilter," just 37 years old. I come from a family of stitchers; my maternal grandmother and great-grandmother taught me to sew, embroider, and make crafty things.

When my husband and I moved from southern California to Maui, Hawaii, in 1992, I had been quilting for about four years. In southern California there were many places to shop for supplies and many women who shared my interest, but Maui was a different story. Then one day a friend told me that a woman she knew was trying to form a guild. At the meeting there were forty women I'd never met, of all ages, all of whom were interested in the fun, lively discussions and friendships that come along with quilting.

A quilt guild is a magical network of women. I say magical because this is a place where you know you are among friends. It is an indescribable feeling, belonging to this tight-knit community of women who do amazing things, with each event bringing everyone closer together.

One of the members is a pediatrician who coordinates the delivery of quilts to critically ill children. These quilts are made and donated by the members, who stitch love into every inch and make them big enough for a child to snuggle into. Also, smaller quilts are made and donated to women who have lost a baby. These "angel wing" quilts are touching reminders of a child no one wants to forget. And recently several women coordinated a quilt for a member's husband who was diagnosed with cancer. His "chemo quilt" comforts him during the ongoing courses of chemotherapy.

These women get together to create works of art, sometimes for a cause, sometimes just for fun, and during this process they create a strong bond of friendship and support for each other. Through the joys and fears, the camaraderie and tears, they stand together.

My grandmothers all passed away before I was twenty years old, and I live thousands of miles away from my mom, so this group of women has become the grandmothers, aunts, sisters, and moms that I need. If women ruled the world, every woman would have a group of women of all ages in their lives whom they could play with, laugh with, and share stories with, while creating a patchwork of memories.

Dianna Grundhauser lives in Maui, Hawaii, with her husband, Bruce. She is an award-winning quilter and is working on her first book, *The Quilting Spirit,* to be published in April 2005.

We'd Extend Care and Compassion to All Members of Our Community

What do we live for, if it is not to make life less difficult for each other?

—George Eliot, novelist

After reading a story in our local paper about a family homeless shelter that was being forced to shut down because the community didn't want it there any more, I decided to take my children on a field trip to a park bench. We arrived early enough to see a homeless woman still asleep, sitting upright on a bench with her hand holding a strap that she'd tied to her shopping cart. A small child leaned against her. We sat down. To pass the time I suggested to my children that we make up stories about the lives of the people we saw in the park that morning—starting with the homeless woman.

My 8-year-old son began, "Just a few years ago that woman worked at the grocery store a few blocks away. She came with her daughter to California from Washington, D.C., to live with her aunt. The aunt died, so now she has no place to live and has to sleep in the park. But the park is nice because it has pretty flowers to look at, and it is sunny and warm."

As the woman woke up and started rummaging through the trash can, my 10-year-old daughter then asked, "Mom, isn't there some place she can go to get food—can we buy them breakfast?" So we continued

The Homeless in Our Nation

- It is estimated that 760,000 people are homeless on any given night, and 1.2 to 2 million people experience homelessness during one year (National Law Center on Homelessness and Poverty).
- A survey of 25 U.S. cities found that in 2000, families with children accounted for 36 percent of the homeless population (U.S. Conference of Mayors, 2000).
- Two trends are largely responsible for the rise in homelessness over the past 15 to 20 years: a growing shortage of affordable rental housing and a simultaneous increase in poverty (National Coalition for the Homeless).
- A Ford Foundation study found that 50 percent of homeless women and children were fleeing abuse (*Women Battering: A Major Cause of Homelessness,* via the National Coalition for the Homeless).

our field trip and went to buy donuts, coffee, and juice for the woman and child.

On the way I explained to my children that we did have a family homeless shelter in our town, but the people in town didn't want those kind of people here any more so they were shutting it down.

My daughter replied, "But where are they supposed to go?"

"Any place but here."

In our society, women have nurtured and fought for what builds family. If we ruled, money that is being spent to kill people in war games would be directed to caring for the people in our own communities who sleep on the cold cement each night and rummage through garbage cans. It may take time before some of our government policies change, but until they do, mothers can teach their children a skill that is so lacking in this material world: the ability to really see and then feel compassion for those less fortunate. Let children experience a new definition of community—looking outside the confines of one's own family and connecting with others.

If we can do this, our children will be armed with the values they need to make different choices when the power does shift to a more nurturing paradigm. They'll know how to build the world we all envision.

Melody Ramos, 42, is a preschool teacher and the mother of two. She and her husband and other concerned community members are raising funds to place homeless families in local motels.

~ Something to Think About ~

A Proactive World Instead of Reactive

I've always wondered why we spend so much money on the results of crimes like domestic violence instead of pouring money into community services that might educate people from age 5 on (way before any abusive behavior would show up) on how to deal with their anger. These programs could be integrated into our school systems and could also include teaching girls and boys how to stand up to someone who is emotionally, verbally, or physically abusive. These are skills all of us could use in dealing with bosses, family members, or spouses. If women ruled the world, I believe we'd be looking at many of our social programs from a proactive, "let's work on it before it breaks" starting point, instead of the reactive approach of fixing things after they're broken—which costs us much more as a society.

—Amelia Rodiguez, 53

Bullying in All Forms Would Be Unacceptable

In violence we forget who we are.

—Mary McCarthy, writer

Everyone should be able to look up at the night sky and see the stars. They should be able to go out in their yard or for an evening stroll down the street and enjoy nature *without* being afraid. Unfortunately, for half of the population in my city, and in many of the cities in the United States and the world, this is not a possibility.

The first time I felt oppressed because of my gender was when I realized that sitting on my porch, looking at stars in my garden, or walking home from class was unsafe for me. A serial rapist was loose in my city, two rapists actually, and though I'd like to think I'm a strong woman, I was terrified.

Months later, both rapists were apprehended, and the hype died down—so everyone forgot about it. Yet I still felt unsafe. These few months of hypervigilance, thinking about these rapes and how the community was responding, helped me to realize that the particular acts of rape were just the tip of the iceberg.

While the rest of the city was focused on increasing police patrols to make neighborhoods "safer" to prevent rape, I was wondering how everyone could ignore the root of the problem, which for the most part was not happening on the streets. People were forgetting the fact that most rapes and violence against women are committed by acquaintances and close friends or family. They were ignoring the social structure that supports this kind of violence against women: pushing, shouting, not knowing when to touch and when not to touch, not being able to take *"No"* for an answer, thinking "No" means "Yes" (or pretending to think so), feeling as if it is all right to make others feel uncomfortable as long as it makes you feel good . . . these are all forms of bullying that our culture often tolerates. These are all forms of aggressive bullying. They are *not* acceptable. By being complacent about bullying, we are *accepting* it. When it is accepted, it becomes part of society's norms.

If women ruled the world, more people would feel free to speak up and confront the aggressor when they saw a woman being bullied in any way, or any person being bullied—young or old, male or female. Too often behaviors such as honking, name calling, and unwanted touches are just laughed off and ignored, but these seemingly small matters contribute to a culture of violence, which frankly *allows* and *feeds into* the problem of aggression and rape. Too many families live with emotional or physical violence that in many cases comes from a perpetrator who has been bullied or abused as a child. As a society, it's time to take a stand against bullying in all of its forms.

Bullying in Our Schools

According to a survey of more than 15,000 public schools by the *Journal of the American Medical Association* in 2001, one-third of respondents maintain that they have been either a victim or perpetrator of bullying. The frequency of bullying was highest among 6th to 8th graders.

NICOLE WINES, 20, is currently living in a small farming community in Slovakia. She is a documentary and experimental filmmaker, media activist, and gardener. Her future plans include starting a rural ecovillage in Slovakia where all forms of bullying will be unacceptable.

Call to Action

Share Your Talents, Barter for Time

- Look for areas of your life where you can trade your time or talent for a service you need, like baby-sitting, housekeeping, word processing, legal or medical services, and so on.
- Start a time credit bank in your community. For help getting started, go to www.timedollar.com or www.transaction.net (look under "time dollars").
- Take a skill survey in your community. Talk to local middle schools, high schools, and elder-care facilities. Find ways to match resources with community needs.
- Persuade local businesses to participate, trading their resources for time.

—Adapted from *Take It Personally* by Anita Roddick

The World Would Be Awash in Pink!

Sorry, but we've reached our quota of pink in the audience today.

—Security guard at the entrance of a stump speech for Arnold Schwarzenegger

If women ruled the world, it would be awash in pink—women in pink boas at a vigil here, chanting in the streets in pink beehive wigs there, carrying pink umbrellas, donning pink body paint, waving pink banners—women in pink you-name-its all over the place.

This isn't your mom's pink. It isn't about Barbie and fluff or playing nice. This pink is about power and action. It's about women coming together from all parts of the country and the world, recognizing that fear-mongering and Code Orange terrorist alerts and duct tape don't make us one bit safer. It's about seeing outside ourselves, recognizing our interconnectedness, and tapping into our compassion. It's about knowing "they" are "we" and the only way to rule the world is to share its wealth and beauty equally—and enough of this whoever-has-the-gold-makes-the-rules stuff.

It's knowing that in standing up for what's right, every now and then you have to get a little outrageous—shake things up a bit. It's understanding that in this mess of a world we live in, sometimes you just gotta find the joy and the fun.

It's realizing there are already a whole mess of women out there right this minute who totally "rule" and are calling for a CODEPINK alert for peace and justice! You rule, too. So what are you waiting for? Throw on some powerful pink clothes and join us.

A New Kind of Alert
CODEPINK uses inventive techniques to get their message out to the public, such as presenting those who are not doing their jobs representing the people—from congresspersons to the media—with pink slips (women's lingerie), demanding they do their jobs or the people will "fire" them (www.codepink4peace.org.).

CAROL NORRIS is a longtime activist, political writer, and national organizer for CODEPINK. When not protesting in her favorite pink beehive wig, she is a psychotherapist and client advocate living in San Francisco, California.

Having a Voice in the Business World

Section 4

Cultural transformation announces itself in sputtering fits and starts, sparked here and there by minor incidents, warmed by new ideas that may smolder for decades. In many different places, at different times, the kindling is laid for the real conflagration—the one that will consume old landmarks and alter the landscape forever.

—Marilyn Ferguson, writer

Introduction

We Would Hold the Door Open for Women to Follow

Wendy Luhabe, social entrepreneur

If women ruled the world, we would not accept limitations. I never accepted limitations as a black woman. I didn't let radical discrimination stop me; instead, I chose how I would define myself. I rejected the norms. I found that I didn't need to be aggressive; all that was necessary was to have a presence. A presence where I could touch people through interaction—if you have an impact on people, you get whatever your intention. But you can't use your skills or even try them out if you never get the opportunity. So whatever situation a woman finds herself in, she simply cannot wait, she must step forward when the space begins to open up. We can only have a presence if we step forward. I was lucky; someone gave me a chance, and this was the stepping stone to the rest of my life—the catalyst for my belief that I did matter.

I had just graduated with a business degree, a rare thing for a young black woman, but still no one would give me a job. I struggled, looking for a solid year after college. I refused to give up or give in; when people offered me jobs beneath my qualifications, I turned them down. I wanted a good job. I knew that if I didn't get the proper start, my self-confidence wouldn't recover. A white guy who had just bought a cosmetics company gave me that chance, without even knowing anything about me—that chance changed my life at the height of the Apartheid regime in South Africa.

The problem I see is that we aren't preparing our young women to be true leaders of the world. The intervention and learning needs to begin at the parenting and education level. We need to create different conditions in our society, conditions that have the potential to produce a different kind of woman. This would mean looking at how we parent, the messages and support we give our girls; it would require a society that honors women and reinforces the positive and powerful principles of the feminine to create balance in the world.

There are women out there who are open to new challenges, who are confident in who they are, and who are willing to lead the way and open doors. Those women need to mentor younger women, and encourage them to be comfortable with themselves. To be the best they can be instead of trying to mold themselves into someone else. When we try to be someone else, we erase our natural gifts and cannot fulfill our life purpose. If we want to be successful, look to women we want to be like, and use their example to ignite our own magnificence. Society has a responsibility to give women a fair chance. If you are a woman out there in the business world who found a way to get that door open, let as many women walk through as possible—don't you dare close it after you.

Namaste, sisters all over the world.

WENDY LUHABE is the chairperson of South Africa's International Marketing Council. She has been recognized by the World Economic Forum as a Global Leader of Tomorrow, as well as honored as one of the 50 Leading Women Entrepreneurs of the World. She is the author of *Defining Moments: Experiences of Black Executives in South Africa's Workplace.*

Our Voices Would Be Heard

Leaders are indispensable, but to produce a major social change many ordinary people must also be involved.

—Anne Firor Scott, writer

The biggest problem in business and politics is that women's voices aren't heard. We need to get more women into positions of power, which includes contributing to corporate boards, sitting on political commissions, and being recognized as experts in our fields.

Yes, this is happening to some extent, but not to the degree it needs to. There are long-standing patterns within our society that have to be confronted and changed before women who have training and qualifications equal to men are going to be given the opportunities in positions of power that they deserve.

To begin with, we have to take a thorough look at the way women are portrayed in the media as "flesh for sale," with a huge emphasis placed on appearance and a frequent focus on breast enlargements and cosmetic surgeries of all kinds. The media communicates the idea that women are not as valued for their intelligence as they are for their beauty, which takes the focus away from women's competence and abilities. It's as if the media's goal is to get women to be so preoccupied with beautifying themselves that they don't have time or energy left to really make an impact in the business or political arena.

That said, it's up to women to take a strong stand on this issue. Women have to begin to recognize the damaging effect this kind of media packaging has on the ability of women to be taken seriously, and they must refuse to support it.

It's also difficult for women's voices to be heard if their work is valued less than men's in monetary terms. Today, women still earn 77 cents for every dollar that men who perform the same jobs earn. One way women are beginning to compensate for this inequality in pay structure is to develop business ownership—which can offer women a bigger piece of the pie. As business owners, women have more control over compensation and personal time, and more influence in decision making. However, businesses owned by women still don't share equally in the economic benefits. Even though women own at least 48 percent of all U.S. businesses, only 3.2 percent of corporate contracts and 2.9 percent of federal contracts go to women. That is why now, more than ever, women need to have more input in the political and corporate agenda to equalize the playing field.

Recently the *New York Times* ran a section on entrepreneurship, and not a single woman was mentioned. A Women in Communications study found that fewer than 5 percent of stories found on the front pages of newspapers were by or about women, and fewer than 10 percent inside the print media were written by or about women. It's as if we aren't seen as an important force in the business world. The disclaimer the media often offer is that the reporters didn't know anyone or have any contacts to interview on the subject.

The same can be said for the political arena. Many political leaders don't call on women to get their input. I recently received an information sheet on a conference about federal procurement. Out of twelve of the featured speakers, eleven were men, and only one was a woman. When President Bill Clinton used to come to New York, which was often, he would ask the opinions of business leaders in the city. You'd always see him surrounded by men in photographs on television.

If we want our voices to be heard, we have to support women in gaining positions of leadership, starting with electing women to positions of power within the government, where they can introduce and help pass bills that support the woman's agenda, especially on economic issues. Women must step up to the plate and be willing to invest their dollars in the political process. Competent, powerful women are out there ready to lead in all areas of business and government. If women ruled the world, our opinions and expertise would be valued and called upon.

DR. FIRESTONE is founder and president of the Women Presidents' Organization for women whose businesses annually gross over $2 million. She was appointed to the National Women's Business Council, which reports to the president of Congress on issues of importance to women in business and which was part of the official delegation to the Overseas Economic Development Council in Istanbul, Turkey.

~

We Would Use the Role of Chief Purchasing Officers of Our Households to Influence Politics and Policy

Women as consumers . . . ought to do what they can do to inform themselves so that they can put their money where their politics are.

—Kim Gandy, President of NOW

Last year, a friend of mine, armed with money to spend and a whole day to shop, was ready to buy some new furniture for her new son. She walked into a high-end furniture store with her baby in the stroller and immediately felt out of place, as the cluttered aisles and tight displays made it impossible to maneuver the stroller.

A saleslady approached and said, "Excuse me, ma'am, but we're really not set up for that kind of thing here." Not only did my friend leave the store, but she recounted her story of unwelcome to so many friends and family members, she affected the store's bottom line.

The truth is, American women make or influence 83 percent of consumer purchases, sign 80 percent of all checks, and make up the third largest economy in the world. Women do rule the world more than they realize, through their economic decision making. If there were more women in business leadership positions, companies might better understand how to communicate with this powerful group of consumers. But the truth is, we have opportunities every day to vote with our pocketbooks.

If women ruled the world, we would embrace our power to influence what is bought and how it is sold to us. We would insist that advertisers portray us realistically by showing images of women young and old, in all shapes and sizes, and from all races and backgrounds—by not purchasing their products or magazines. We would ideally affect packaging, politics, and message, leaving no woman to feel pressured to conform to an unrealistic female form portrayed in an ad.

Our Power as Consumers

Women currently purchase or influence the purchase of 80 percent of all consumer goods, including stocks, computers, and automobiles. According to research by *Business Week* and Gallup, by 2010, women are expected to control $1 trillion, or 60 percent of the country's wealth.

If women ruled the world, shopping would be fun. We would make sure that salespeople in stores offered to hold our babies while we shopped for furniture, rather than telling us they weren't equipped for a stroller. Customer service would cater to our needs as shoppers. Aisles would be wider. Lighting would be more flattering. Dressing-room attendants would be more attentive. And retailers would understand that sometimes we shop for great bargains, but we also shop to relieve stress, socialize with friends, find great treasures, or just to escape.

If women ruled the world, we would recognize and capitalize on our influence as the chief purchasing officers of our households, the primary consumer targets of mass media advertising, and advocates for retail customer service that follows the Golden Rule.

CARRIE MCCAMENT is the managing director of Frank About Women, a marketing-to-women consultancy that specializes in helping companies reach out to women consumers. She is also the multitasking CEO of her family of four boys.

Call to Action

Exercise Your Influence

- Purchase environmentally sound products.
- Make organic food choices when possible.
- Support educational products instead of commercially driven products.
- Discriminate in TV viewing.
- Buy magazines with advertising and messages that support women.
- Support small, independent business owners.

Stay-at-Home Parenting Would Be Counted as Paid Work (with Retirement Benefits!)

At work, you think of the children you have left at home.
At home, you think of the work you've left unfinished.
Such a struggle is unleashed within yourself. Your heart is torn.

—Golda Meir, Israeli prime minister and politician

Before I had my first child, I imagined I would have a full-time, professional, paid job my whole life. I would wake up, have coffee in the still morning, shower, and head off to work in some quiet, cozy office. Looking back, I realize that, while I had assumed I would have children, I never envisioned children in my life. I never saw myself mothering.

Then I had my son, and I could not leave him.

I stayed home to mother him for a year and a half. It was a wonderful, terrible time. My husband and I had no money beyond our minimum mortgage payment and basic bills. We had nothing in the bank, so I fretted and cried at night, afraid.

Eventually I could not take the stress of worrying over our finances, so I took a job. It was wonderful. I worked part time, my sister watched my son for an affordable rate, and I was able to establish a bank account with an actual sum in it for our little family.

Then I had my daughter. Fast forward to right now.

I am a three-headed monster: stay-at-home mother, marketing professional, and writer. I like to think I have this arrangement parceled neatly into thirds. But wait. What about the early mornings and evenings I spend at the computer with my paid work? So, half-marketing professional, quarter-mom, and quarter-writer?

Well, that can't be, since a quarter of a mother could not breastfeed an infant and potty-train a toddler at the same time with any success. Count night feedings. That brings it to something like five-eighths mother, three-eighths marketing professional, one-tenths writer, which does not add up. Could I really equal more than the sum of my parts? How do I tally the time spent writing with a baby in my lap,

A Progressive Constitution

The Venezuelan constitution is considered one of the most progressive in the world. References to the president or any governmental official are recognized in the male and feminine form, and each political party is required to reserve 30 percent of its candidates positions for women. In Venezuela's new constitution, domestic work is recognized as worthy of Social Security benefits. Specifically, it states:

> The State guarantees the equality and equitable treatment of men and women in the exercise of the right to work. The state recognizes work at home as an economic activity that creates added value and produces social welfare and wealth. Homemakers are entitled to Social Security in accordance with law. (Article 88)

answering phone calls from my boss? What about when the baby comes with me to the office? Is pumping milk behind my desk while making phone calls an act of mothering? Do I make subtractions for the times I miss a cue while deeply involved in my writing, and my toddler pees his pants? If I pick up children's books at a trip to the library I originally planned for work research, how much do I deduct from my timesheet?

Like it or not, a mother has a job. A mother with a paid job has two jobs—at least. I am considered a lucky mother, with an understanding boss and now the financial luxury of knowing I can walk away if I cannot take the demands and my children will still have a warm bed and meals, at least for awhile.

But if I exercise this choice and stay home with my children, do not whisper behind my back that I am wasting my education to run a household. If I call in to the office because the baby has an ear infection, do not suggest I am not carrying my load. And if I keep my position and place my children in the trust of a loving care provider, do not conclude that I love them any less. By judging my choices, you vilify me, no matter which path I follow. If we do this, we succeed in creating a society where no woman is 100 percent supported, where no woman's decision to work or to stay at home is the right one.

If women ruled the world, we would support the demands of motherhood and fatherhood—gasp—maybe even consider it a job! Perhaps if health care, Social Security credits, and retirement programs will be were, these choices would be easier to make, and more of them would be made in the best interest of the family.

Jo Phillip is a 30-year-old mother of two with a couple other jobs on the side. She chases her dreams, loves her family, and struggles for balance from a home base in Neenah, Wisconsin.

Why Family and Medical Leave Matters

According to Equal Rights and Economic Opportunity for Women and Girls (www.equalrights.org):

- 46 percent of the total U.S. labor force are women.
- 64 percent of mothers with children under age 6 were working or looking for work in March 1998.
- 64 percent of Americans said that it is getting harder to balance work and family.
- 72 percent of men and 63 percent of women say that they will probably need to take family or medical leave during the next 10 years.
- 84 percent of employers find that providing family or medical leave causes benefits such as positive returns on investments in leave programs, offsetting the costs.
- Two-thirds of employees believe that leave for family and medical reasons was not an unfair burden on coworkers.
- 62.5 percent of women leave-takers received some pay (compared to 70 percent of men), and less than 50 percent of leave-takers who were young (age 18 to 24), who were never married, who had less than a high school education, or who had a household income of less than $20,000 received any pay during their leave.
- 89 percent of parents of young children and 84 percent of all adults support expanding disability or unemployment insurance as a vehicle for paid family leave.
- Some states have proposed expanding existing unemployment insurance or temporary disability insurance programs to provide partial wage replacement for employees on family and medical leave.

Call to Action

Put Parenting on the Social Agenda

- Question parenting options and nontraditional roles.
- Ask employers and negotiate for family-friendly work policies (for both parents!).
- Educate yourself about the possibility of Social Security credits for stay-at-home parents (www.mothersoughttohaveequalrights.org).
- Vote for representatives that support subsidized day care and paid leave for parents of newborns.

The Work Versus Family Trade-Off Wouldn't Exist

"Feelings of worth can flourish only in an atmosphere where individual differences are appreciated, mistakes are tolerated, communication is open, and rules are flexible—the kind of atomosphere that is found in a nuturing family."

—Virginia Satir, writer and therapist

Back in the mid-1980s I had to leave the *New York Times* after my son was born, because in those days the paper offered no alternatives to a full-time job. Since my husband had just started a company and was tied to a 24/7 schedule, I had no choice but to quit my job if our new baby was to have any time with his parents. Things are better now at the *Times,* but I have the impression that there won't be significant changes in corporate America until more mothers are at the very top of organizations, as opposed to being merely high-ranking females in a male-dominated environment.

When an active, involved mother—or father—is the ultimate boss, two things often happen. First, the worker norm changes, and the typical worker doesn't mind being seen as someone with family responsibilities, instead of pretending they have no life outside of work. This shift in perception makes life much easier for conscientious parents who in the past might have lied, saying they were leaving work for a doctor's appointment when they were in truth attending a school event.

And second, leaders with hands-on child-rearing experience themselves appreciate the fact that parents bring a set of transferable skills to their work. These include ways of dealing with difficult, immature people; the ability to work under pressure amid constant interruptions; knowing how to motivate others; and a healthy sense of perspective.

When business begins to acknowledge the importance of workers being active and responsible parents and supports these roles through reduced work weeks, on-site child care, and job promotion regardless of parental status, we'll begin taking steps to reduce the extreme work/family trade-off that exists in the United States.

ANN CRITTENDEN is an award-winning journalist and author, most recently of *The Price of Motherhood.* She lives with her family in Washington, D.C.

~ Something to Think About ~

Parental Leave Policy

The Family Leave and Medical Leave Act (FMLA) was enacted in the United States in 1993 and provides employees with up to 12 weeks of unpaid leave to take care of their own serious health conditions, or care for children, spouses, or parents with serious health conditions, or to care for newborn, newly adopted, or foster children. The FMLA applies to those who work in companies of at least 50 employees and who have worked at least 1,250 hours in the previous year. The policy further does not include any income replacement or pay during the leave. Policies of most other Western countries provide longer periods of leave and often wage replacement or supplemental income—and they tend to be more universal in scope, including maternity, paternity, and parental leave.

- Canadians qualify for 17 weeks of maternity leave—fifteen weeks in which they receive 55 percent of their prior earnings—and ten weeks' parental leave, when workers can receive 55 percent of prior earnings.
- Many European countries provide even more benefits to parents. In Denmark, there is a policy of 28 weeks of maternity leave, during which workers can receive 60 percent or their prior earnings, and one year of parental leave, when parents can claim 90 percent of the unemployment benefit rate. In Norway, the policy is 52 weeks of parental leave at 80 percent of prior earnings and a two-year child-rearing leave, paid out at a flat rate. And in France, there is a 16-week maternity leave at 100 percent of prior earnings and a parental leave until the child is 3.

Being Happy Would Be a Career Goal

Happiness is a state of consciousness which
proceeds from the achievement of one's values.
—Ayn Rand, writer

I've taken a nontraditional approach and navigated through my career by asking myself the following questions frequently: Am I happy? Am I making progress? Am I content? If the answer is "No" to any of these, I start making changes. We all underestimate the power of change to inspire and ignite our career direction and business choices. I continually look at where I want to be five years out and then set my goals accordingly. We have to ask ourselves honestly, "Is this the right track for me?" We can't be afraid to look at the cost or benefit of personal growth compared to the prestige of our position or financial rewards.

Women on the career fast track face tremendous competitive pressure within any organization or industry. So we have to work hard but also recognize and address our personal issues fearlessly and compassionately. The pressures of competition can be positive; they get creative juices flowing, which helps us resolve problems that may seem unsolvable. Women inherently are good in management roles because of their nurturing skills. However, as managers, we tend to want to build consensus before moving forward, and if we don't get everyone on board we feel frustrated. Though 80 percent of the time, drawing others out and building consensus is the right approach, 20 percent of the time listening to your instincts even if they're not in line with consensus is the right thing to do. When I've reached difficult decisions using my instincts, I have felt great relief and a sense of inner peace. Suddenly I feel confident in my ability to defend myself and my ideas, which leaves a lingering feeling of empowerment. I feel energized in a way not experienced before, and thus my personal growth is accelerated and I feel invincible.

Of course, while sailing through your personal life, all days are not the same. I know I can't feel happy in my career all the time. At times there are tough people to deal with, projects with impossible deadlines, disappointments and stressful situations that can be unbearable—but I look at my happiness on the average. If I start to feel bogged down (usually a situation I've created myself because of my own expectations) for extended periods of time, I must rectify the situation. Women who lead tend to be ambitious. I'm ambitious—so checking in on how I'm feeling helps me to know when to stop pushing myself. Sometimes you just have to have hope, a belief in yourself, that it will all turn out!

VINITA GUPTA is founder and chair of Quick Eagle Networks. She founded it as Digital Link in 1985 and as CEO led it to a successful initial public offering. She is an engineer from UCLA, a mother, and a wife. She serves on the board of the Palo Alto Medical Foundation and as chair of its Research Institute.

The Corporate Model Would Expand

All my life, I wanted to be somebody.
Now I see that I should have been more specific.

—Lily Tomlin, actress and comedian

By all societal standards, I had made it. I was indeed "somebody." I had the salary, the stock, and the title in a Fortune 500 company to prove it. Yes, I was one of those young, fast-track women and by my mid-thirties had accomplished what most corporate folks deem success. Yet this somebody that I had become came with a price tag; my work identity was wholly tied in to who I was. I was so steeped in proving that I was enough—enough as a corporate officer, enough as a business developer, enough as an engineer, and enough as a woman in a male-dominated company—that I was unaware of the toll it was taking on the real me.

I became my competition. I did not laugh easily; I put on weight; I suffered from migraines regularly and found myself surrounded only by work-related activities. Any restlessness or anxiety I felt at the time, I directly attributed to my need to prove myself even more. It became a vicious cycle of needing to prove and then needing to be validated—that, of course, is how I knew I won. This was certainly not the "somebody" I had always wanted to be.

Unbeknownst to me at the time, and just underneath the 12- to 14-hour workdays, the leash of my Blackberry and cell phone, and the far-too-regular coast-to-coast business trips, lurked the whispering voice of the "somebody" I had long since forgotten. It was the chronic migraines that first enabled me to hear it. It was in the dark and quiet migraine recovery space that I began to listen to this whisper of a voice—first, to help relieve the migraines and then to help recreate my life.

Corporate success, although it paid the bills and met some of my intellectual standards for success, was not my passion, nor was it my path. Success was tied too tightly to winning at any cost. Life became more about living to work as opposed to working to live. When I allowed myself to reflect on this as a woman, I became very concerned with where my life was going. Does the American dream really come at this cost? How and when did I buy into this so-called work ethic? I wondered if there were other corporate women out there who felt the same isolation that I sometimes felt. Why didn't we seek each other out? I decided to look for my own answers.

For the past four years, while still working part time at the Fortune 500 company, I focused my studies in the healing sciences and arts—massage, intuitive tools, energy healing. In addition to learning just how tied I was to my work identity and how afraid I was of the fact that I might not be anything else if I were not my successful "work self," I learned that I had not embraced my own femininity. At some level I considered it not relevant to my success in the existing corporate model. What a revelation! If I felt this way, how could men not? What an educational opportunity for all of us!

I began to live my newfound ethos, and my life changed. I realized that I did not have to adjust the corporate model; it is the corporate model that needs adjusting. Women, as a group, must ensure that diversity in leadership in corporate America prevails; our call to service is our own personal contribution.

June 1, 2004, was my last workday at that Fortune 500 company. I am forever grateful for my tenure there; I found pieces of myself that I might not have otherwise found. My journey continues; I have cofounded a healing-science company that will be launched in Fall 2004 to help women *and* men bring more of what they want into their lives. Maybe then, we will all be a little more *specific* about the "somebody" we want to be.

NANCY PABERS, 43, currently resides in the San Diego area with her husband. She served as a vice president of corporate development for a Fortune 500 company for nearly ten years. She has a Ph.D. in Healing Science, M.S. in Management Science, and a B.S. in Mechanical Engineering.

We'd Create a Community of Support

The time came when to remain a bud was
more painful than to risk to blossom.

—Anaïs Nin

One day I received an e-mail—"Please pass along to all the young women in your life." The e-mail described the goal of five women—ages 45–70—who were all very successful in each of their chosen fields. They decided that they wanted to give back and create a workshop for women ages 25–35 to coach and mentor them on their life choices. The universe had answered my call for help! I had just accepted a job in San Francisco, and although it was a great opportunity to enter into a field I was passionate about, I was terrified of moving to a new city where I had no support and no community. I would be starting from scratch.

I called the institute and begged to be included in the program. I packed my bags and spent a month in San Francisco before driving to Ashland, Oregon, for the workshop.

Nine of us came together for four days of talking, listening, and working on ourselves. Our mentors were all caring, compassionate women. We listened to their stories and shared our own. We created a circle of support, where you could listen openly—not give suggestions but just listen and then tell your own story. Many of the things we were going through and struggling with, our mentors had experienced twenty years before. Not a lot had changed; some things were easier, but others harder. The true gift was taking four days to work on yourself. It's not often that women get the chance to be in a safe, supportive space where others authentically listen. We talked about the lack of mentors many of us had had prior to this. We learned the power of setting intentions and the ways to develop a stronger sense of our internal self. This circle of support gave me the greatest gift—the confidence to listen to my inner voice in all situations, to trust my intuition, and to know that the answers I seek come from within myself and not from my family, friends, teachers, or coworkers.

This community of women continues to support me through both career success and frustrations. A job I loved ended as the company was sold and moved to another state. The next job lasted a year—but I eventually left because the company did not uphold many of the values I hold true. To leave a well-paying job in a bad economy—with nothing else lined up—took having faith in myself and trusting all that I had learned from my mentorship experience: the importance of self-trust and listening to my inner voice, and the need to create a community that sustains me and continues to help me grow.

If women ruled the world, we would all have these learning circles available to us. Old and young would gather together in support, sharing our stories and learning from each other.

HEATHER MCARTHUR, 32, is a freelance editor living in the San Francisco Bay Area with her husband.

Female Athletes Would Be Treated the Same as Male Athletes

It is possible to read the history of this country as one long struggle to extend the liberties established in our Constitution to everyone in America.

—Molly Ivins, columnist

I guess I should be appreciative, even ecstatic, at the opportunity to attend the University of Michigan on a water polo scholarship. However, now that I am living this dream, my enthusiasm is waning as I see men's teams' posters slathered on the walls at every student bar, cheap eats place, and corner liquor store. Where are the posters for the women's

Women and Sports

Title IX states, "No person in the United States shall, on the basis of sex, be excluded from participation in, be denied the benefits of, or be subjected to discrimination under any educational program or activity receiving Federal financial assistance." Times have changed dramatically since Title IX was signed as law in 1972. But still, according to a NCAA 2000 Government Accounting Office report, women's teams receive less than 40 percent of recruiting dollars and less than 43 percent of athletic operating dollars. For more information on women's sports, check out www.womenssportsfoundation.org.

teams? I wish I could enjoy a nice lobster and filet mignon like the football team instead of consuming wilted lettuce and undistinguishable packaged meat in the cafeteria. I'd love to get a good practice time in the pool, instead of being excluded from 12 P.M.–5 P.M. classes while the men's swim team claims the pool's most convenient hours.

Last week the school paper announced it would have to increase the price of tickets for football games in order to fund the athletic department. The second sentence of the article quoted a male student demanding that the school get rid of "stupid girl" sports, especially girls' water polo—he claimed that water polo was taking up all the school's funds by recruiting girls from California. That guy was talking about me—a girl from California, playing what he called a "stupid girl" sport. It's ironic that he would say this considering that women's water polo awards the least number of scholarships even though it is one of the largest girls' team. The uniform is about an eighth of the cost of one football pad, and still it is a women's team that is blamed for the lack of athletic funding. No one would ever demand that the football team stop staying at the Beverley Wilshire during the Rose Bowl.

It hurt me that a fellow student wanted to cut my program simply because of my gender. When I voiced my anger to some of the older girls on the team, their response was, "It's just the way it is; get used to it." But I don't want to get used to it; I want this to change. I wake up at 6 A.M. four times a week, lift weights three times a week, and spend more than 20 hours in the water practicing. I attend numerous team meetings to go over plays and I give up my social life to travel every weekend to compete—why shouldn't I be treated as well as a male athlete?

A pessimist might believe it's just the stark reality: "You ladies may have Title IX, but you can't change how an institution treats you." But I am not a pessimist; I'm living my dream, the dream I've had since I was eight years old, when I watched my idol, Summer Sanders, win an Olympic gold. From then on I believed I could do it, too, be a world-class athlete, and I am not about to let a group of naysayers destroy my dream. I am an optimist.

I'll do my part to make this change happen—I'll cover the city's cafés, stores, restaurants, and bars with our team poster, send out e-mails to get students to attend our games, and walk with confidence as I wear my Water Polo sweatshirt. And I'll commit to heart the words of Maya Angelou:

> You may trot me down in the very dirt, but still like the dust I rise. Does my happiness upset you? Don't you take it awful hard, cause I laugh like I got an oil-well pumping in my living room. You may shoot me with your words. You may cut me with your eyes. And I'll rise. I'll rise. I'll rise.

Wesley Ellison, 19, is a sophomore at the University of Michigan. She's an avid reader, art history buff, travel enthusiast, and participant in many sports who excels in creative writing and cultural studies.

We Would Celebrate Our Ability to Do Anything

Women must try to do things as men have tried.
When they fail, their failure must be a challenge to others.

—Amelia Earhart, aviation pioneer

I've been meeting a colleague for lemon tarts on Friday afternoons for the last year or so. We talk about everything from our passion for cats to the overcrowded freeways to the genocide aftermath in Rwanda. At one point in our conversation, I tell her that I'm working on my pilot's license, and how yesterday I popped open the window in order to breathe in the loamy smell of cracked earth and creosote bush as I was swooping in for a landing.

"Oh my goodness!" she said. "I could never fly. I don't know how you do it."

"It's just practice," I assured her. "You get good at it."

"No," she insisted. "I'm not smart enough to fly."

I'm not smart or brave enough to fly? Is this what women believe, truly?

I've come to realize over the months I've been taking flying lessons that most of my female acquaintances are deeply intimidated by flying (despite the accomplishments of the wildly popular Amelia Earhart). They come up with dozens of reasons why they could "never" do it: I'm afraid of heights, I've got children, I have no time to learn with managing my home, I want to stay on firm ground. And women who do take to the air are instantly labeled brave, fearless, or intrepid. We couldn't be ordinary women; we must be a different breed; under our silky skin, we must be warriors.

On the other hand, when I mention my flying aspirations to my male counterparts, their eyes sparkle. A man at the library recently said to me, "I've always meant to get my pilot's license." Indeed, for men, perfectly ordinary men, flying is something they've been meaning to do but haven't found the time for—yet.

If women ruled the world, being a woman pilot wouldn't be so extraordinary. There would be no need to join the Air Force or go to war in order to fly. We wouldn't feel compelled to emulate men—wear a baseball cap or combat boots, chew bubble gum, or spit tobacco in the gutter—in order to belong to the flying community. Flying would be an everyday sort of thing for women, like cooking a meal or giving the baby a bath.

Women in Aviation

On November 2, 1929, 99 licensed women pilots came together for the mutual support and advancement of aviation. The Ninety-Nines is now an international organization with more than 6,000 members from 35 countries (www.ninety-nines.org).

DOMINIQUE MCCAFFERTY, 30, is a government documents librarian at the Riverside Public Library in Riverside, California. She currently lives with her boyfriend and their two cats in San Bernardino, California.

We'd Have More Women Conductors

There are very few jobs that actually require a penis or vagina. All other jobs should be open to everybody.

—Florynce Kennedy, lawyer and activist

Think of the last time you went to a concert of classical music. All of the instrumentalists assembled on the stage in their elegant black and white, the orchestra tuned to the oboist's A, and—as a hush fell over the hall—a dashing figure in tux or tails strode across the stage to great applause. How surprised would the audience be if the commanding figure were a woman rather than a man? After all the strides that women have made in nearly every field since the early 1970s, conductors of all major orchestras—worldwide—are still overwhelmingly male.

When I first applied to a New York conservatory as a graduate conducting student, the single question I was asked by my future male instructor was, "How often do you rush to the net when playing tennis?" I wondered at the time what that had to do with conducting. Even before that, when I was a senior in high school and concert mistress of our orchestra, I looked forward to the customary privilege, accorded to the person with that position, of conducting a piece at the last concert of the year. Much to my surprise, our conductor, whom we all revered, presented me midyear with a mandolin in lieu of the conducting gig. The honor of conducting the orchestra had always gone to a male, and he argued that it would be hard on the players if it went to me. I didn't even squawk at the time (it was 1956).

In the late 1970s I worked with a collective of women to produce an issue on "Women and Music," for a publication in New York. It was a heady time for feminists. We were a real "crossover" group of musicians; we came from the world of folk, pop, and classical music. Meetings (several evenings every week) were lively. The idea of whether a good feminist vision should include more women conductors, perhaps many conducting the same orchestra, or whether the notion of one conductor virtually ruling over as many as a hundred skilled musicians was antithetical to all we believed was a topic of discussion.

More than 25 years have passed since we produced our issue on "Women and Music," and the list of highly acclaimed (and regularly employed) women orchestral conductors can be ticked off on the fingers of one hand. I still wonder why that is, with all the talented female musicians out there. Perhaps instructors are still handing the conducting gig to their male students, or maybe women are responding as I did when I earned the right to be mistress of the orchestra but agreed to step aside and say nothing. If women ruled the world, I believe no thought would cross our minds as to what is appropriate for a woman to do or be—we would embrace our talents and claim our accomplishments.

Musical Facts

- In 1997, the American Symphony Orchestra League listed 425 professional orchestras; only 29 had women music directors or principal conductors.
- Vitezslava Kapralova was a Czech composer and conductor in the early 1900s. The Kapralova Society promotes women composers and conductors with a comprehensive list of resources worldwide (www.kapralova.org).
- Nadia Boulanger was the first woman to conduct the Boston Symphony and the New York Philharmonic.

BARBARA LACHMAN, 65, has written two books about Hildegard of Bingen and one about William Blake's wife, Catherine. She's a certified teacher of the Alexander Technique and director of choral music at Rockbridge County High School in Virginia.

Businesses Would Focus on Employee Needs

Figure out what your most magnificent qualities are and make them indispensable to the people you want to work with. Notice I didn't say "work for."

—Linda Bloodworth-Thomason, writer and TV producer

A teacher once said to me, "If you live your life like you have cancer, you will never get it." That's how I've chosen to live my life and run my company. If one of my employees is stressed or unhappy to the point that she needs to take days off, hates coming into work because of a dispute with a manager or coworker, or shows up just because she needs a paycheck—then she might as well stay home in bed. Why *not* set up your life (and company) in a nurturing way—the way you would if you were living every day to its fullest?

Twenty years ago I was a single mom, working as a waitress. Today I own my own trucking company with 46 nurtured employees and am the mother of seven children from the ages of 5 to 30 years old! I've covered the walls of our building with inspirational murals and messages. Mothers can bring their infants to work and attend to them next to their desks. Older children can be brought to work with a sitter, since we've dedicated 10 percent of the building space to a playroom and outdoor play area. We hold staff meetings outside, around a fire pit. I try to encourage my employees to reach personal goals they set through the many programs we offer, including a weight-loss incentive where they get paid real money for every mile they walk and pound they lose. I walk the floor every day to talk with my employees, and I make sure that there is a birthday card in the mail with a crisp $20 bill for every family member.

We all need the companies we work for to survive, but work cannot become more important than our family life. Nobody in my company is allowed to work on Saturdays or Sundays, and I make sure the building is empty every night by 7. If you have a family, you need to be there for them—I want my people to go home and have dinner together. If you don't have a family, you still need time for a personal life. We all need space away from work to participate in activities, develop hobbies, enjoy a sport, or garden—this makes for much happier and more relaxed employees.

By setting up my company this way, I get workers who are passionate, men and women who give of their time and of themselves because they're on the bandwagon to make this company the best it can be. You get a sense from everyone here that they are valued and cared for, because I do truly care. Employee turnover is lower, which costs the company less in training and fosters a feeling of family.

When I get an idea for a new incentive or a way to make my company better, I don't have committee meetings for months to figure out if the plan is feasible or who might benefit—I just say, "Let's do it." That's a woman's way—we're always in a building, changing, growing, let's-do-it-now, things-can-be-better mindset.

If women ruled the business world, work would be just work, a part of our lives—and we'd all know how to contribute to creating work environments that nurture ourselves without feeling guilty. If you're going to be a single parent or married and a parent, and you're working, the load is so tremendous—you have to take time for yourself. As women, we feel so guilty about that. We choose to put others first, nurturing them; we put the life jacket on our kids while we slowly drown. Nurturing ourselves as women has to become a priority. Once we understand this and begin to implement it in our family lives, it becomes easier to demand this same respect of self and family from our employers.

CAROLYN GABLE is president of New Age Transportation in Zurich, Illinois, and founder of Expect a Miracle Foundation, which funds extracurricular activites for children from single-parent families. She's the mother of 7.

We'd Compete to Cooperate, and Everybody Would Go Home in a Pink Cadillac

The real success of our personal lives and careers can best be measured by the relationships we have with the people most dear to us—our family, friends, and coworkers. If we fail in this aspect of our lives, no matter how vast our worldly possessions or how high on the corporate ladder we climb, we will have achieved very little.

—Mary Kay Ash, entrepreneur

When you're tracking a beast or ambushing an opponent, a command-and-control leadership model gets the job done. If you're going to arm guys with spears, the last thing you need is for them to start voicing their own opinions. But when you find yourself alone with a pack of screaming cave kids and a fire that needs stoking, and your food for the season is dependent on the bag of seeds in your hand, you learn to employ more collaborative methods. It's no coincidence that men took their previously successful organizational models into the modern workplace.

Had women been in charge of the workplace from the get-go, things would be different. Husbands would not be allowed to take paternity leave, they would be *required* to. Personal expression would be encouraged, company restrooms would stock free tampons, and cover-up stick in every shade from ebony to alabaster would be an office expense just like the coffee.

But the biggest change women would make is in the way businesses are organized. Instead of being structured around who's in charge of whom, organizations would be arranged around the actual work to be done. Just like a well-run PTA, companies would operate as an ever-moving network of committees; well-respected, peer-chosen leaders would ask people how they wanted to contribute, and assignments would be made accordingly; rewards would be based on contributions, not senior management face time; and everybody would get misty-eyed at the end of a job well done.

Ladies, it's time to let the men be men. They're the only ones who are really good at it, and if their way works for them, let them have at it. Communication and commitment are a woman's forte, and when we apply our feminine wiles to the world of work we create our own environment for success.

A more cynical woman might tell you that the ability to track large game has seen a real decline in marketability, whereas influencing others is a skill that will take businesses into the future. But instead I'll just ask you to contemplate two companies: Enron and Mary Kay.

Who's filed for bankruptcy, and who's driving a convoy of pink Cadillacs all the way to the bank? Women do rule the world; we just don't know it yet.

LISA EARLE MCLEOD is an international speaker, syndicated columnist, and the author of *Forget Perfect*.

~ Something to Think About ~

JUMPING AT OPPORTUNITY

A few years ago I happened to be in my boss's office when she answered the phone and began discussing what sounded to me like a job opportunity within the company we worked for. We had been talking about a small project I was working on when the phone rang, so I sat patiently finishing up some notes, but in truth I was eavesdropping on the conversation. I wrote down the name of the person, took a few notes on the description I overheard, and headed directly back to my computer to search the company files for that particular first name. Ten minutes later, I went into my boss's office, told her that I couldn't help but overhearing—and that I wanted that job. I had the confidence I could do it, and I was ready for a promotion. Up to that point in my career I was the one opening the doors for my coworkers, pointing out their strengths and politely saying, "After you," whenever I heard of an interesting new job opportunity—because I believed that if the job was right for me, someone in the company would offer it to me. I got the job, and I love the job—and I learned that day that you have to jump at opportunities.

—Jenny Urbain, 32

Business Would Be More Fun!

To love what you do and feel that it matters—
how could anything be more fun?
—Katharine Graham, *Washington Post* editor

The man at the trade show was busily handing out brochures about his company's product—a new bookkeeping software program. As the owner of a bookkeeping service, I was interested in getting his information, so I walked over and asked for a brochure.

"This is the hottest new product on the market," he informed me proudly.

"Great!" I said happily. "I own a bookkeeping service, and I'd love to look at it. Maybe we can network and send each other business," I suggested with a smile.

He looked down at me with disdain. "Oh, no," he smirked. "We're going to put you out of business!"

Needless to say, I didn't enjoy that response very much. I said, "Oh, no you're not," turned away, and deposited his brochure in the nearest trash receptacle.

That was a long time ago, and I don't remember his name or his product. But he certainly didn't put me out of business. I think if women ruled the world, there would be less of this kind of "dog eat dog" competition. The spirit of consensus, working together and networking to achieve goals would be more prevalent. This is not to say that all men want to put everyone else out of business, but it seems more acceptable and expected for men to have the goal of being number one regardless of the cost. In the traditional, male-dominated approach to business, shutting everyone else out of the marketplace is like winning a big race—as if second place is a bad place to be. Or to be a small business only means you didn't have the guts, drive, determination, intelligence, or talent to be a big one. The way the world works from this perspective is that the winner of first place gets all the glory, fame, rewards, and money. Those in second, third, and fourth place are seen as losers.

I later sold that bookkeeping business to start teaching financial stress reduction workshops. I wanted more freedom and flexibility, so I set up the business my way—small. I teach my classes at home: I put the coffee on, people come, I teach them, I take the coffee off. If I want a vacation, I take it. I don't make as much money as Anthony Robbins, but so what? I'm living my dream life. I think if women ruled the world, there'd be more businesses based on my small and happy model. And there'd be lots of time to play, to laugh, to enjoy the wonderful world we live in and the people we live in it with.

I don't care what my number is. I feel like a winner.

CHELLIE CAMPBELL is a professional speaker and author of *The Wealthy Spirit: Daily Affirmations for Financial Stress Reduction.*

Women-Owned Businesses Thriving

- As of 2002, there were an estimated 10.1 million privately held businesses in which a woman or women own at least 50 percent of the company.
- The workforces of women-owned firms show more gender equity: women business owners overall employ a roughly balanced workforce (52 percent women, 48 percent men), while men business owners employ 38 percent women and 62 percent men on average, according to the U.S. Chamber of Commerce.

We Would Have a Safer World

Women are one-half of the world but until a century ago . . . it was a man's world. The laws were man's laws, the government a man's government, the country a man's country. . . . The man's world must become a man's and a woman's world. Why are we afraid? It is the next step forward on the path to the sunrise, and the sun is rising over a new heaven and a new earth.

—Martha Thomas, educator, in an address to the North American Woman Suffrage Association, 1908

As a trial lawyer and past president of the Association of Trial Lawyers of America, I see many products put on the market that maim and kill. Women and children are especially susceptible to being injured by these products.

Among those that have done grave damage to women are the Dalkon Shield, DES, breast implants, the diet drug fen-phen, and hormone replacement, as well as drugs and devices that are less gender specific.

Because most of corporate America is still run by men, many companies do not conduct sufficient research into the effects of pharmaceutical products on women, or they tend to ignore the results and downplay adverse reports. If more women were involved at the highest levels of industry, more thought, research, and work would be devoted to protecting the health and safety of women. More women in decision-making positions would assure more attention to the potential effects of products on women: women would influence the selection of products to market, the depth of research, and in the review of clinical data. Women would not be ignored.

Unfortunately, in our society women and children continue to be the most vulnerable—the least able to pay medical bills and absorb the loss of earning capacity, which still is typically less than that of men. They have less of a voice and less power and, therefore, are more at risk because of dangerous products that put profit before people.

When corporations fail to make products as safe as they could and should, the law must protect consumers. The civil justice system and the citizen jury—our friends, neighbors, and coworkers who do their patriot duty by hearing all the evidence and making intelligent judgments—help level the playing field. These foundations of our democracy allow the least powerful young woman to hold accountable the wealthiest and most powerful corporation.

Mary E. Alexander, J.D., M.P.H., is an experienced trial lawyer, past president of the Association of Trial Lawyers of America, and recipient of many distinguished honors; she has bben named one of the Top Ten Trial Lawyers in the Bay Area and one of the Top 100 Most Influential Lawyers.

More Research Needed on Products for Women

- A series of twelve deaths due to miscarriage-related infections in the early 1970s drove the popular Dalkon Shield IUD off the market. These deaths could have been prevented had the manufacturer tested the product more thoroughly and listened to warnings from both a co-inventor and a quality control supervisor at the plant that produced the IUD.

- Although silicone breast implants first came onto the market in the early 1960s, they were not even reviewed by the FDA until 1991, after nearly one million women had them put in. These silicone implants could not be determined to be safe or unsafe, yet reports of illnesses in women with implants were being published in medical journals. It would be another decade until saline-filled implants would be reviewed, and the FDA approved two manufacturers despite extremely high complication rates during the first three years.

- DES (diethylstilbestrol) is a synthetic form of estrogen, a female hormone. It was prescribed between 1940 and 1971 to help women with certain complications of pregnancy. When given during the first five months of a pregnancy, DES can interfere with the development of the reproductive system in a fetus. In 1971, DES was linked to an uncommon cancer (called clear cell adenocarcinoma) in a small number of daughters of women who had used DES during pregnancy. This cancer of the vagina or cervix usually occurs after age 14, with most cases found at age 19 or 20 in DES-exposed daughters.

- Hormone replacement therapy (HRT) is the combination of estrogen and progestin hormones generally prescribed to relieve menopausal symptoms, reduce risk of osteoporosis, and reduce risk of cardiovascular disease. During a clinical study in 2002, the National Institutes of Health's (NIH) Women's Health Initiative (WHI) found an increased risk of invasive breast cancer from HRT. The increased risk of breast cancer appeared after four years of hormone use. After 5.2 years, estrogen plus progestin use resulted in a 26 percent increase in the risk of breast cancer—or eight more breast cancers each year for every 10,000 women. The WHI also found that HRT could increase a woman's risk for heart disease, stroke, and pulmonary embolism.

Call to Action

Support Product and Consumer Safety

Before buying a product or service, make sure you've checked for negative reports.

Good sources to try are:

- Nonprofit resources (www.ConsumersUnion.org)
- Government resources (www.cpsc.gov)
- U.S. Consumer Product Safety Commission (www.fda.gov/medwatch/safety.htm)

If you'd like to file a complaint to the Federal Communications Commission, go to www.fcc.gov/cgb

We'd Value the Health of Our Children More Than Big Business

It is strange that the more we learn about how to build health, the less healthy Americans become.

—Adelle Davis, nutritionist and writer

I am sitting in a doctor's office while my 3-year-old begins to run around in circles, faster and faster, until I am dizzy just watching him. But my son never gets dizzy, just as he never stops speaking to himself in a low, droning voice. If I listen, I know that I will hear dialogue from *The Lion King,* perfect down to the exact tone of Simba's roar. When the last line is said, he will simply start from the beginning again. He says nothing else.

The doctor enters, an older, bespectacled gentleman. He watches Dillon for a moment, then looks at the chart he is carrying. After asking me some pointed questions, he solemnly lowers his glasses and says that terrible word, the one that still haunts me on dark nights when I cannot sleep: *autism.*

Many years have passed since that day, when the world I thought I lived in disappeared forever, to be replaced by one full of behavioral and occupational therapy, speech lessons, and special diets. Dillon eventually stopped spinning and reciting movie scripts and learned more appropriate behavior. As the years rolled by, the cause of his autism remained a mystery, even as more and more children succumbed to the same diagnosis.

Although some argument remains, most experts agree that the rate of autism in American children has increased from 1 in 10,000 in 1970 to 1 in 166 by the late 1990s. Although the reasons for this increase are not yet certain, one theory has been gaining credibility, as more and more scientific studies point to a correlation between a mercury-containing preservative used in vaccines, called thimerosal, and an increase in neurological disabilities in children, particularly autism.

Thirmerosal, a drug which is 50 percent mercury by weight, has been added to childhood vaccines since the early 1970s, despite the fact that the FDA never conducted any long-term safety trials on its usage. By the time the FDA finally tallied the total amount of mercury being given over a period of time in 1999, they discovered that these children were receiving more than 100 times the EPA's safe limit for mercury. That same year, the FDA required the removal of thimerosal from all over-the-counter drugs. The government did not require that it be removed from vaccines.

In 1999, the Centers for Disease Control (CDC) became concerned over data that pointed to a statistically significant relationship between thimerosal and neurological problems, including autism, in a large group of children. The findings were released privately to several government agencies and the vaccine's manufacturers at a closed conference at the Simpsonwood Conference Center in Georgia in 2000. Participants were concerned that this information might have a negative impact on America's immunization program, so, instead of publishing this data and alerting parents to the potential danger this preservative posed for their children, the agency chose to consider it "embargoed information." The findings were not released until July 2001, when the CDC was forced to disclose them under the Freedom of Information Act.

Even then, the agency did not require the removal of mercury from childhood vaccines, though it recommended that the use of thimerosal by vaccine manufacturers be phased out. The intervening years produced a slew of scientifically rigorous studies pointing to a connection between mercury and autism, including a groundbreaking study by Dr. Mady Hornig of Columbia University that replicated the thimerosal regime given to humans in mice, finding that mice developed a disorder similar to autism. But only on April 5, 2004, with the introduction of legislation to ban mercury from vaccines in the U.S. Congress, was any significant government action to limit childhood exposure to this neurotoxin proposed. Most state agencies estimate that it will cost between $5 and 10 million to care for each of the autistic children currently growing older within their social services systems. With the numbers of chil-

Thimerosal-Containing Vaccines

- Tom Vilsack, the governor of Iowa, signed into law in May 2004 a bill that effectively bans the administration of thimerosal-containing vaccines to children. This is the first state to do so.

- "A day after I ordered it (thimerosal), I received a frantic call from the FedEx office. The woman on the other end said that they would not be able to deliver thimerosal to my home. She said, 'It's too dangerous—it needs to be handled in a secure lab with protective clothing.' She wasn't overreacting, though—there was an incident a few years ago when a researcher from Dartmouth spilled a drop of dimethyl mercury (the mercury in thimerosal). They did everything they could to treat her. She died a few months later. This is the same stuff we are injecting into our kids."

  —Dr. Mark Geier, vaccine researcher, in "The Rise Against Mercury" by Sarah Bridges (*Seed* magazine)

dren developing autism and other neurological problems continuing to rise, the total cost to the government will be in the trillions. Thus, a tiny savings by vaccine manufacturers (big business) could turn out to be a huge cost for American taxpayers.

No woman would ever look into the eyes of her child and decide to trade that child's future for monetary savings of any amount. Nor would she advocate the injection of a known neurotoxin into that child's tiny body without testing the effects first. And once those effects were suspected to be toxic, no woman would have hesitated to insist on the toxin's removal. We will all pay a great price for this serious breach of the public trust.

DENISE JOSEPH, 42, is the mother of three. Her youngest son is autistic. She spends her volunteer time working with an autism research organization with the hope of shedding light on the vaccine issues confronting our nation.

The Wisdom to Seek National Solutions

Section 5

Women need to see ourselves as individuals capable of creating change. That is what political and economic power is all about: having a voice, being able to shape the future. Women's absence from decision-making positions has deprived the country of a necessary perspective.

—Madeleine Kunin, former governor of Vermont

Introduction

We'd Put a Compassionate Face on America

MEDEA BENJAMIN, cofounder of Global Exchange and CODEPINK

I've been working for world peace for twenty-five years, but September 11, 2001, was a watershed. I was horrified by the 9/11 attack, and then horrified by the way the U.S. government responded to that attack by bombing Afghanistan and Iraq. I felt the need to show the world that not all Americans believe that the way to deal with the taking of innocent lives is to take more innocent lives.

I traveled with a group of women to Afghanistan during the initial bombing campaign because I was so upset at the way the bombing was being portrayed in the U.S. media. We didn't see the blood, grief, and agony of war. Instead what we saw on TV and in the news looked like a Nintendo game.

When our women's group arrived in Afghanistan, we saw entire villages that were wiped out, women and children killed, maimed, destitute, orphaned, and widowed. We came back to the United States to urge the media to talk about the civilian casualties, to "put a human face on the war," but we found no interest. Meanwhile, the rest of the world saw the horror of "collateral damage," and they decided that Americans only care about their own lives.

So we organized another delegation of people to go back to Afghanistan, this time comprised of people who had lost family members on 9/11. We had a father who lost his 20-year-old only daughter on the United Airlines flight over Pennsylvania. The first day we were in Afghanistan, that man met a woman who lost her 20-year-old son to a U.S. bomb. The American man said that when he looked into the Afghan mother's eyes, he felt a bolt of electricity go through him. They couldn't talk because of language barriers, and he couldn't hug her because of religious rules, but the bonding was deep, and he's never forgotten her. This man has since gone back to Afghanistan to help build a school for girls. That trip, and subsequent ones, helped show Afghan people that there are indeed Americans who grieve and feel deep apology for their losses.

When the United States invaded Iraq, we made a similar trip there, this time with U.S. military families who had loved ones serving or killed in Iraq. Again, we experienced the people's anger and their anguish.

As a nation, we are now seeing the effects of a policy that believes it is right to use violence to counter violence, hate to counter hate. The result has been both the bombing and shooting of innocent civilians, as well as the torture and abuse of prisoners. This has stoked anti-American sentiment around the world, making us less safe here at home and abroad.

I remember, after 9/11, reading the daily tributes in the *New York Times* to those who died. I would cry every time I read one of these "Portraits of Grief," as they were called, because in just a few paragraphs you got a feeling for who this person was, what they did for work and for pleasure, whom they loved and left behind. For a brief moment, these victims came alive. You felt connected to them; you felt the tremendous pain that ripples down to their family, coworkers, friends, and neighbors—the hundreds of people affected for each person who dies.

When we kill people in other places, we need to somehow see their portraits. We need to hear, for example, about the beautiful 9-year-old Afghan child Freshta, who, her mother told us, was always laughing, smiling, and dancing around the house, especially when her father would bring her pomegranates from the bazaar. Her dream of becoming a teacher was cut short one night when an errant U.S. bomb hit her house, crushing her and her baby brother while they were sleeping.

We need to experience the same level of compassion for each innocent person killed; we need to dissect this terrible term "collateral damage." We need to understand that more innocent people died during our attacks on Afghanistan and Iraq than on 9/11. We need to understand that *war* is terror.

If compassionate, informed women ruled the world, we would capture and try those suspected of terrorist attacks, but we would not bomb entire nations. We would support international law and the United Nations, promote an end to all weapons of mass destruction (not selectively telling some countries they can't have them and then continuing to build them ourselves). We would take much of our incredibly bloated military budget and put that money into activities at home and abroad that would make people's lives better—primary education, health care, clean drinking water. We would encourage Americans to learn more about the world by interacting in a positive way with the other inhabitants of this planet—learning second languages in school, forming exchange programs with other cities, schools, churches, and mosques. If powerful, creative women ruled the world, we would humanize the horror of war, humanize the victims of war, so that no government would look to war as an option.

MEDEA BENJAMIN is founding director of Global Exchange and is also the cofounder of CODEPINK: Women for Peace. For more than 20 years, Medea has supported human rights and social justice struggles around the world.

All People Would Vote

When good people in any country cease their vigilance and struggle, then evil men prevail.

—Pearl Buck, writer and missionary

In the United States of America, women comprise more than 50 percent of the potential electorate, so there is a good argument to be made that women rule the U.S.A. Yet I look at the government and I don't see women's power reflected back to me. We've had the vote for more than eighty years, but frankly, U.S. policy has been less reflective of my values in this new century than it has at any time during my voting life. A policy of conducting preemptive war, backing out of international treaties designed to reduce the proliferation of nuclear weapons, assaulting our environment, diminishing our civil liberties, and taking out loans on our future that puts Social Security, our economy, and our children in jeopardy—these are not policies that reflect my values or that work for my family and our future.

Voting- and Women-Related Resources on the Web

Center for the American Woman and Politics (www.cawp.rutgers.edu)

Emily's List (www.emilyslist.org)

League of Women Voters (www.lwv.org)

National Women's Political Caucus (www.nwpc.org)

Vote, Run, Lead (www.voterunlead.org)

Women Leaders Online (www.wlo.org)

Women Matter (www.womenmatter.net)

Women's Action for New Directions (www.wand.org)

Women's Campaign Fund (WCF) (www.wcfonline.org)

Women's Voices, Women's Vote (www.wvwv.org)

Working Women Vote (www.goodgovernment.org)

To find the voting records and information for candidates, visit www.vote-smart.org.

War, poverty, and injustice would cease to exist if women voted against politicians who backed these policies. It is time for women to engage in the political dialogue full on, encouraging and supporting leadership that our whole nation can be proud of. Our political system has become increasingly hollow, overly influenced by corporations and money. A mass infusion of citizen energy is a grand way to cure this. Franklin D. Roosevelt was famous for saying, "You've convinced me, now make me do it." Our best politicians desperately want us to "make them do it." Without citizen support, they are dangling in the breeze. It is our job to connect with one another and provide these leaders with the people power they require to pass legislation that will move us toward our ideal world.

In September 1998, six months into the Clinton impeachment mess, my husband and I were frustrated by the paralysis of the government, particularly the failure of our elected leaders to get back to the business

Missing at the Polls

According to the U.S. Census Bureau, Americans aged 18 to 24 vote less than any other age group. In 2000, only 32.3 percent of the voting population between 18 and 24—and 43.7 percent of those 25 to 34—turned out to vote. By contrast, 66.8 percent of voters aged 55 to 64 turned out. In the 2000 presidential election, 68 percent of married women went to the voting booth, but only 52 percent of single women cast a vote. Sixteen million unmarried women were not registered to vote in 2000, and nearly 22 million unmarried women did not cast ballots on Election Day.

of governing. In response, we sent out a one-sentence petition to fewer than 100 friends and family members: "Congress must immediately censure President Clinton and move on to pressing issues facing the nation." Registering www.MoveOn.org, we set up a simple Web site, and more than 100,000 people signed our petition in a week! That was when I realized the great potential ordinary people have for transforming our political ills. I've learned that citizens will step forward in huge numbers to engage in the political dialogue when given a meaningful way to do so.

In 2000, only 51 percent of the potential electorate voted. There is a huge opportunity and challenge here for everyone who wants to see change; if the 49 percent who didn't vote for one reason or another get out and vote for people and causes that will better this country, change will happen. The challenge part: Get out there and find a way to inform that 49 percent on issues at stake in this country, then convince them that their vote can truly matter, and then drag them to the polls to take a stand!

JOAN BLADES is the cofounder of MoveOn.org, a civic action group dedicated to giving ordinary citizens a voice. She lives in northern California with her family.

~ Something to Think About ~

Election Tactics

What bothers me the most about our electoral process is how potential candidates spend millions of dollars to go on the air to bash their opponents. What kind of role modeling is this for our children? I try my best to teach my children certain values. Be kind to others and walk away when someone doesn't say nice things. Ignore them. Then I see the leaders of our country displaying such childish behaviors. The money spent on this could be used to better our children's future instead of to fund a display of finger pointing.

—Karen Utech, 40

We'd Support Women in Leadership Positions

The day will come when men will recognize woman as his peer, not only at the fireside, but in councils of the nation. Then, and not until then, will there be the perfect comradeship, the ideal union between the sexes that shall result in the highest development of the race.

—Susan B. Anthony, suffragist

We need more women in political leadership. This is about making the pie bigger, bringing in new points of view and experiences. It's about bringing the best of both male and female influences to the table for the betterment of all. It's about giving a voice to the solution you believe in. If women ruled the world, the average person would have a stronger voice than the rich and powerful.

The new model of great leadership would be a more feminine, collaborative style, where the leader is a relationship builder who sees the value of different points of view. This new leader would be at the center of concentric circles of environments. For that is the nature of women: we function at the center of the worlds of family and friends, business and the community, the nation and the world. It's all about inclusion, across lines of authority, and not keeping "different" people out. If women ruled the world, the laws of the United States (and other countries) would respond better to the needs of the people and be negotiated in a more collaborative and less overtly partisan, competitive way. A good example of women working toward this goal of collaborative solutions is the group of female representatives in the Senate who meet monthly to negotiate legislation they can all support, setting partisanship aside.

Apathy is not an option, it's a danger. Apathy means we don't care. Those who do not vote have no say—about who holds office, about taxes, about the health-care system, about transportation, about threats to clean air and water, about labor laws, about outsourcing, or about the government's response to terrorism and economic issues. We have to get out there and vote more women into positions of political leadership. We live with the consequences of public policy choices every day. It's about being actively engaged, taking responsibility for being a part of your world, and not just watching passively.

My great-great aunt was a news reporter who interviewed the suffragist Susan B. Anthony on several occasions. Miriam Michelson was taken by Anthony's tenacity, strength, and clarity of purpose. Here's an excerpt

The State of Women Leaders

The 2000 U.S. Census Bureau reports that as the rates of women voting increased in the past decade, so did a number of social changes for women, including educational attainment and labor force participation.

- In total, 73 of the 535 members of Congress (both houses) are women.
- Of the 12,000 members of Congress elected in the history of the United States, there have only been 215 women.
- There have only been 25 women governors in American history, including those serving now.
- Of the nearly 600 people who have served in the president's cabinet or as cabinet-level officers since Washington's term, only 29 (or approximately 5 percent) have been women.
- No woman of color has ever been governor of a U.S. state.

—From Vote, Run, Lead

from one of those interviews, from *Failure Is Impossible, Susan B. Anthony in Her Own Words*, published in 1985, written by Lynn Sherr: "I wish I were a Susan B. Anthony. . . . I should like to feel that I was really of as much consequence in the world as Miss Anthony feels herself to be—and she is not a bit conceited, either. It must be a fine thing to believe that you are leading a great movement that will triumph and prove to the immense benefit of the world."

If we remain silent, after all that our sisters endured in the hard-fought battle culminating only in 1905 with the 19th Amendment to the U.S. Constitution, we are abdicating control over the major issues of our lives, squandering a right that people all over the world risk their lives to earn. There is an army of women out there who have Anthony's tenacity, strength, and clarity of purpose; we just need to support them in gaining leadership positions.

JOAN BRYNA MICHELSON, 47, is president/CEO of Michelson/Cooper Marketing in Las Vegas and Public Policy Chair, National Association of Women Business Owners (southern Nevada).

CALL TO ACTION

Promote Women in Leadership

The 2000 U.S. Census Bureau reports that as the rates of women voting increased in the past decade, so did a number of social changes for women, including educational attainment and labor force participation. The White House Project is an organization dedicated to promoting women in positions of leadership (www.thewhitehouseproject.org). They have many resources and suggestions for taking action, from inviting a woman you know to run for office to supporting elected leaders. What can you do?

- Evaluate newspapers, magazines and Internet articles: Support candidates who are addressing issues that are important to you.
- Send letters to local media management with a list of women leaders and experts for future stories.
- Most importantly, get out to vote! Register to vote at www.workingforchange.com/vote. Go to www.fec.gov/votregis/vr.htm and print out copies of the National Voter Registration form, which is good in most states. You can also request an absentee ballot by contacting your local county or city election official; go to www.fvap.gov/links/statelinks.html for the official site of the secretaries of state and/or directors of elections in your community.

There Would Be No Unplanned Pregnancies

No woman can call herself free until she can choose consciously whether she will or will not be a mother.

—Margaret H. Sanger, nurse and birth control reformer

Imagine a method of birth control that would prevent all unwanted pregnancies. There may be work ahead for biochemists to implement this plan; however, if fluoride can be added to our water supply, why not a spermicide? Here's how it would work. The water supply throughout the United States would contain a spermicidal element that makes every man who drinks the water sterile. This spermicide would need to be specific to the human male and have no effect of any kind on any other life form. Since water is unavoidable, the entire male population would be infertile.

In order to conceive a baby, a couple would be required to appear before a magistrate on two separate occasions at least six months apart. At the second appearance, the man would be given a three-month supply of pills that would neutralize the spermicide.

The two people who want to have a baby need offer only IDs with a photograph and date of birth (each must be at least twenty-one). They need not be married. They need not testify as to occupation, mental status, previous children, income, criminal record, health, addiction, or anything else. There will be only two requirements for parenthood: adulthood and a more-than-fleeting desire to have children. The magistrate's only function would be to record the couple's two visits and to dispense the pills.

The no-parent child might vanish, since people too irresponsible to care for children would also probably be too irresponsible to show up twice before a magistrate. Abortion would only be sought in cases of a blighted fetus or an endangered mother. Sterilization would no longer be necessary. Other forms of birth control would only be used when traveling abroad.

This new method of birth control does not curtail civil liberties or reproductive rights; it merely introduces something familiar to anybody who has applied for a license, a membership, or a job—the waiting period. So maybe this is a fantasy! Many positive societal changes begin with an innovative idea carried out by open-minded people who set out to solve a problem.

EDITH PEARLMAN has been writing for 35 of her 67 years. She has won many prizes. Her third collection of stories, *How to Fall,* will be published by Sarabande Press in February 2005.

Male Birth Control Pill

- A male birth control pill, proven to be 100 percent effective in clinical tests conducted thus far, is set to go on the market in 2005. Just like the female birth control pill, it must be taken every day in order to work properly.
- Planned Parenthood provides information and access to health and reproductive services (www.plannedparenthood.org). The Reproductive Health Outlook is another organization that provides up-to-date summaries of research, programs, and clinical guidelines related to reproductive health topics. (www.rho.org)

Family Court Orders Would Be Enforced

I have come to believe that the one thing people cannot bear is a sense of injustice. Poverty, cold, even hunger, are more bearable than injustice.

—Millicent Fenwick, U.S. diplomat and congresswoman 1975–1982

When a marriage ends in divorce, a court order is drawn up and agreed upon by both parties. Frequently, the noncustodial parent decides not to follow the court order, by not paying child support or deciding not to be involved in the kids' lives at all. My question is, Why do we create court orders if they can't be enforced without further court action or great expense? Parents spend months and sometimes years in court trying to get their ex-spouses to do the right thing. Yet often, in the end, the noncustodial parent gets away with negligence anyway.

I've spent two years in court, while my ex claimed unemployment and switched from a $30/hour job to a $7.50/hour job just to avoid child support. He was the classic deadbeat dad. In theory I did end up winning: the judge decided that my ex-husband did indeed change jobs intentionally, so the child support settlement was based on what he could be making. But in practicality it means nothing. I have no way to collect it, no influence or rights that can require the father of my children to do the right thing.

If women ruled the world, there would be significant consequences and easy ways to collect money owed that would not involve going back to court numerous times, paying lawyers for years, and silently cursing the system.

Often, family members help support a noncustodial parent by hiding the money being earned so it can't be collected, or they pay living expenses so the person can get a lesser-paying job in preparation for a court appearance. If the courts went after extended family member's assets and wages, we might see more child support being paid. Let the other members of the family feel the financial burden, and have them put pressure on the parent to meet his family responsibilities. Perhaps money could be deducted from a debit or charge card every time it was used, and that money would go directly into an account to pay off back child support.

Unpaid Child Support
The Federal Office of Child Support reports that $92.3 billion in accumulated unpaid support (up from $88 billion in 2001) is due to almost 20 million children in the United States. Visit the Association for Children for Enforcement of Support (www.childsupport-aces.org) for resources.

The system does not work in the best interest of the children. If one parent can walk away while the custodial parent is stressed and overwhelmed, something is out of whack. The law isn't protecting those it should—children. If women ruled the world, court orders would be quickly, easily, and fairly enforced in the best interest of children, without further litigation, hiring of private investigators, or depletion of assets while one parent struggles to collect child support from the other.

Karen Utech is a single mom raising two kids. She is a special education teacher living in Colgate, Wisconsin.

~ Something to Think About ~

Our Welfare System

The social welfare system, born in the 1930s as palliative for the previous century's economic anguish, is showing its age in a number of probably unforeseen ways. The existence of a baseline safety net, hung no matter how low, has created a stratum of society that's both welfare-dependent and welfare-wise. Publicly, we say the net is there so no child, no family falling into poverty smashes irreparably on the hard cement of hunger and homelessness. The conservatives among us like to assert their own economic virtue by insisting that no single mother should reside long on the public rolls, that it is more noble to clean other people's toilets for minimum wage than it is to spend one's productive hours caring for one's own children. In fact, economic policy, ethics, and psychology intersect at just this point. Today's well-loved child grows up to be tomorrow's effective citizen. Better we support mothers in toilet training, not toilet cleaning. Today's welfare dollars should be an investment in our common future, reflecting our insistence that our children must fare well.

—Joyce Thompson, 55

Special Education Would Truly Be Special

Theories and goals of education don't matter a whit if you don't consider your students to be human beings.

—Lou Ann Walker, writer

I'm sitting in a windowless room with a nervous parent of a special-needs child beside me. Across from us are those school district personnel responsible for this child's education, joined by a new addition to their team: the school district's attorney. The child's mother twists a piece of tissue in her hands, which only moments before she had been crying into. She has never been in such a hostile situation before, but I, as an attorney-advocate for special-needs families and a parent of an autistic child myself, have seen this scenario played out over and over again. As we sit in this stuffy room, the school district's attorney begins to play the "game."

When the Individuals with Disabilities Education Act (IDEA) was reauthorized in 1990, its purpose was to provide disabled children with an appropriate education specifically tailored to their particular needs. Under this law, school districts are required to identify those children within its district who have special educational requirements and then to meet those needs. Lack of resources cannot be used as an excuse for noncompliance. Yet federal and state governments provide inadequate funding to implement these costly programs, leaving the school districts in a difficult position.

Required by law to educate these children but lacking the resources to do so, many school district administrators have learned to play an insidious game with the parents of their disabled students. The game goes something like this: If a parent comes to the school district unaware of the specific provisions of IDEA and trusting the administrators to inform them of their child's rights (the most common scenario), the district will often choose to steer the parents into well-established, less expensive programs, whether or not these are in the best interests of the child. Parents are often not told about every program available to their child, in order to keep the number of children with access to the more costly programs low. In such cases parents, making decisions based on limited information, often do agree to the school district's recommendation, even if the program is not adequate for their child's particular needs.

On the other hand, if parents enter the school district well informed about IDEA and what their child is entitled to, they stand a much higher chance of gaining an appropriate education for that child. But this is actually where the game gets interesting. There are many ways to delay or even prevent the acquisition of services. For example, if a parent wants a new service, the district can require that the child be tested to see if he or she is eligible for that service. If the parent does not trust an internal, school district assessment to be unbiased (sometimes a valid concern), they must seek outside testing, which they pay for themselves. If, after this testing, the school district still refuses to provide the services, the parents must then choose between providing the service at their own expense or taking the district to court. Either way, getting what the child needs costs time and money.

Thus, the system is biased in favor of affluent, well-educated parents, who have the knowledge and the resources to fight for their disabled child's education. The poor, the middle class, and those less educated are generally given less for their child because they often don't have the time or the money to challenge the system.

This truly tragic result is an outgrowth of the education system under IDEA. Many school districts simply don't have the resources to give all of their disabled children an adequate education. Yet the administrators cannot use this as an excuse when denying services. They are forced to play the game in order to conserve enough resources so that the well-informed parents who know that their child cannot be denied services based on cost will get what they ask for.

The parent I am sitting with is one of the lucky ones. She can afford to pay for me to fight for her child so that he gets the services that he needs and deserves in our affluent society. No child left behind, the president has said, and so it should be.

If women ruled the world, the education of our weakest children would be a high priority, supported not just in words but with national resources, for women understand that a society should be judged by how its most powerless members are treated. Then we could end this terrible game of fighting for scarce resources which is played out every day in special-education offices around the county, and return to the real goal of all education: preparing our children for the future.

Julia York, 43, is a writer and attorney-advocate for families with disabled children. She holds advanced degrees from Columbia University and the University of California, Hastings College of the Law.

The Individuals with Disabilities Education Act

In 1975, Congress agreed to provide 40 percent of the national average per-pupil expenditure to states and local school districts in order to pay the excess costs of educating children with disabilities. This goal has rarely been met. In fiscal year 2004, IDEA was funded at $10.1 billion, approximately 18 percent of the total that Congress committed to pay. An amendment to the Senate bill reauthorizing IDEA passed on May 13, 2004, proposing that Congress "fully fund" special-education programs by adding $2.2 billion annually and so meet its failed obligations. Instead, the Senate adopted another amendment that would authorize discretionary funding to reach the 40 percent target by 2011. The House of Representatives passed a similar measure last April. Thus, Congress will continue to defer paying the full cost of educating the disabled, even as the number of such children increases daily.

—From Autism Society of America e-Newsletter, May 15, 2004

Video Violence Would Become Flower Power

There is a long macho tradition in this culture that pronounces certain kinds of violence as perfectly appropriate.

—Sarah J. McCarthy, writer and critic

Pow! Blam! Gunfire, followed by the nauseating crunch of breaking bone. More gunfire, followed by a scream and the soft "splat" of viscera spattering against the wall. And this is just Level I. Welcome to children's entertainment, circa 21 century: video games for kids who just aren't getting enough death and destruction in their lives.

I became conscious of these games when I moved to New York and began walking home from work. My path takes me past an electronics store in midtown Manhattan, where a gargantuan television screen in the window runs a 3-D video game in an endless loop. The villains vary—one week it's skeletons, the next it's Nazis—but the story line remains: Good conquers evil, in the goriest manner possible. In a dubious attempt at equal opportunity, for a few weeks the bad guy was a bad girl, a Barbie-proportioned animatronic wet dream clad in latex and thigh-high boots. I knew she was evil because her face kept dissolving into a fire-breathing skull. No glass ceiling here; women can be just as bad, and in high heels, too!

Particularly disturbing is the fact that this violence is marketed toward kids. This store, for example, has placed its television directly at a child's eye level, and I've often had to thread my way through knots of small boys—I call them "Joeys"—grouped on the sidewalk, staring, transfixed, as bones crunch and eyeballs squirt from sockets. I've talked to the proprietors several times. The interactions go something like this:

STOREOWNER: May I help you?

ME: Yes, about that video in the window—

STOREOWNER: Ah! Chill 'em-Kill 'em-Blast 'em-Waste 'em, our best-seller. Which version would you like?

ME: Actually, I was wondering why you're showing it at children's eye level.

STOREOWNER (suddenly losing his ability to understand English): Video? For your children?

This goes on for several minutes. The manager is called over. He pats my shoulder, oozing solicitousness. I feel patronized. I also feel unpleasantly self-righteous. He has to make a living, after all, and he'd probably go out of business if he didn't stock junk like this.

Me (wanly, losing the battle): Would you want your children to walk by every day and see this stuff?

Storeowner (breaking into a smile): Ah, my children! Here, let me show you a photo. So you want to buy video?

If women ruled the world, we wouldn't have to take shop owners to task, because the video industry that has Joey directly in its crossfire, so to speak, wouldn't exist. Or it might exist, but in a very different form. I have a fantasy of subverting video violence with unexpected and unsettling beauty, à la *Fantasia* or *Yellow Submarine.* In this fantasy, I write a computer virus that encodes itself into the Chill 'em-Kill 'em-Blast 'em-Waste 'em series. Joey races home from school for his daily fix, logs on, and begins to navigate through the barren video landscape. What's that sound? It's a demon, fangs bared. Joey aims his virtual revolver and presses the trigger. Poof! Out pops a flower from the barrel of the gun. Taken aback, Joey loads his Uzi and fires, only to watch his foe dissolve into iridescent soap bubbles. Joey looks on, helpless, as grass grows and trees start to flower on the screen. More demons appear, but every time Joey lands a punch or fires a shot, another flower unfurls. He's created a garden! If he's quick-witted, he'll realize that he's got a whole new set of skills to learn—climatology, soil typing, cultivars—and a whole new crop of enemies to contend with. An unexpected freeze, after all, could demolish an entire bed of bulbs, while planting a sun-loving tomato plant in a shady area could

TV Viewing and Our Children

According to a study reported by the Associated Press, television viewing may play a role in the increase in attention-deficit disorder in children. Research found that each hour of TV from age 1 to 3 years amounted to a 10 percent increased risk of attention problems by age 7. Other studies linked television watching by very young children to obesity and aggressiveness.

By age 18, a U.S. youth will have seen 16,000 simulated murders and 200,000 acts of violence, according to the American Psychiatric Association.

The ESRB rating system (www.esrb.org) helps parents and other consumers choose the games that are right for their families.

spell disaster for the crop. Not to mention the bane of every gardener: pests. Blister beetles, giant root borers, fiery searchers, sharpshooters, flesh flies, skeletonizers: I challenge any video connoisseur to battle these demons.

It's just a dream, I know. I broached my video-garden fantasy to a Joey I know, a 10-year-old boy who has recently discovered video violence. After he finished laughing, he picked up his joystick and gave me a look. "That's so . . . for girls," he said pityingly. Exactly.

Juliet Eastland, 35, lives in New York City. Her writing has appeared in *bitch* magazine and other print and online venues. She would rather be playing the piano than playing video games.

Call to Action

Watch Less Television

Demonstrate selective TV viewing by watching *programs* rather than TV. Suggest alternatives and provide opportunities for your family to enjoy other forms of entertainment. Make a list of all the things you like to do but never have time for—and encourage all family members to spend their time on sports, hobbies, or with friends.

- Next time you feel like watching TV, turn on the stereo instead, and do something around your house you've been putting off but need to do. Notice how good you feel afterward.
- Watch at least one episode of the programs you allow your children to watch. When you see a violent incident, discuss what caused the character to act in a violent way.

- Ensure younger children are viewing age-appropriate shows.
- Keep a record for one month of how many hours your family watches TV. Then have a family meeting to discuss other ways to spend time.

Questions to ask about violence in video games: Is the violence rewarded or punished? What are the consequences? How graphic is the violence? Is the violence against humans or inanimate objects? Is the violence sexual?

—From the National Institute on Media and the Family (www.mediafamily.org)

We Would Portray Real Women in Advertisements

The real thing creates its own poetry.

—Anzia Yezierska, novelist

I have just about abandoned magazine reading as a pastime. Some of my favorite magazines have folded, and the majority of the most popular women's magazines are generally offensive. Offensive because they seem to suggest that ordinary-looking women are not exciting enough to interest readers, that a woman's goal in life is to focus on appearance as opposed to knowledge, wisdom, or joy in life.

As a woman in my 40s I have found only one and a half magazines (*More* and *O: The Oprah Magazine,* part of the time) that regularly offer articles about, and advertising containing, women in my age bracket. I know I am not the only 40-year-old woman in America, but I also know that in America the media is fixated on youth, and we all—the 40-plus women included!—buy into the idea that youthful appearance is the be-all end-all goal. This is ridiculous.

Truth in Advertising

About-Face (www.about-face.org) combats negative and distorted images of women in the media through education and activism.

Everyone is moving in the opposite direction—away from youth. We age. Youth is not something to be worshipped and yearned after but rather enjoyed at the time it is experienced.

As a young woman in my teens and 20s I used to read magazines from page 1 to the end, closely examining the women in both the articles and advertisements. I continually compared myself to them, wishing I could be more like them. I think of young women now, reading those magazines as I used to, torturing themselves with, "If only . . ." and "I wish . . ." when comparing themselves.

As an educated woman, I realize that the media has a heavy influence on the public, but these are "women's" magazines—bought by women—with many advertisements promoting diet products, Botox,® and "corrective" surgery.

Where are the older, typical women in these publications? Would we not be as motivated to attain happiness if guided by a woman who was 5 feet 4 inches and 150 pounds? Would not a 60-year-old woman be able to offer us wisdom and thoughts on what is to come in the years ahead? Must we all focus on yesterday, wishing we were still 25—or at least still looked 25? What future are we promoting for our daughters, nieces, and young neighbors?

If women ruled the world, we would portray realism in advertising, along with interesting and intellectually stimulating content within the media. We would be content with our appearance and therefore have time and energy to focus, instead, on internal growth or community and political responsibility. As it is, we sometimes seem so focused on what we don't have, or what we should be striving for, that we wind up feeling diminished instead of using our time and energy to make real changes in the world.

DIANNA W. ALLEN, 41, is the single mother of a 16-year-old son, is employed in an autistic support classroom, is involved with a youth criminal diversionary committee, and is working toward a master's degree in Counseling.

CALL TO ACTION

Promote Positive Images of Women

- Purchase magazines that depict women of all ages and races. Don't buy magazines, or support companies or media outlets, that promote unhealthy, degrading images of women.
- Write letters or send e-mails of support to companies that depict diverse women in their advertisements. Let them know you notice and you care. Write letters to magazines and advertisers whose ads are offensive to women and girls.
- Inform companies that portray negative images of women how you feel, via e-mail or letters. Encourage them to change course.
- Stop insulting yourself. Stop complaining about your weight. Stop putting yourself down. Adult women are trained to complain and apologize about their own appearance. Stop—our daughters are listening and learning.

- Teach your children from a young age a new definition of what it means to be a strong woman. A strong woman is smart and brave. Make sure to ask your daughter what she thinks about the female characters on TV or in movies.

We'd Shift How Sex Is Portrayed

Pornography is not about sex. It's about an imbalance of male-female power that allows and even requires sex to be used as a form of aggression.

—Gloria Steinem, writer, journalist, and founder of *Ms.* magazine

Pornography ruined my marriage. It captured my husband's attention and demanded to be his first love and his first priority. It seems like he was always unable to account for his time. A trip to the hardware store would take all day. Washing the car sometimes lasted until midnight. I wondered for a long time if there was another woman. But it was worse than that: He was having an affair that consumed his mind.

"Are you sure all you did was wash the car, honey?" I questioned one midnight.

"Yes, honey, that's all I did."

But I know the truth; I took an odometer reading before he left. "You traveled over a hundred miles to go to the car wash, which is just 2 miles around the corner," I said.

I felt dirty. This time there was no need to grit my teeth and take a firm stance in preparation for his accusations of my paranoia. This time was-different. I had proof.

"It's not another woman, you have to believe me," he begged.

"It's still pornography, isn't it?" When there was no reaction, I continued, "You have to leave. I can't do this. I can't put the kids through this again."

Seven years ago, my husband left to wash the car, and I filed for divorce. Pornography—and his obsession with it—stole my life, my hopes, dreams, and my marriage. Once my husband exposed himself to the images of porn over and over again, his ability to love me and make love to me slipped away. He expected that I would play out the sordid sex acts and creativity that he had viewed. The more pornography he viewed, the more deluded his requests were, and the more deluded he became about what a "real" relationship and genuine intimacy were.

I was finally so repulsed that I was no longer able to engage in a healthy sexual relationship with my own husband. I couldn't compete with the images that were in his mind. Enjoying the physical sensation and pleasure of lovemaking triggered his memory to recall the last pornography that he viewed. When we were intimate, his mind left me, and his heart followed behind. He never returned to me.

It would have been easier to say that my husband was an alcoholic. It's the same sick addiction, but pornography has so much more shame and consequence. I suffered quietly, and I didn't want people to know. In spite of that, it just kept leaking out and I couldn't contain it. It poisoned my soul. I wonder how many other people are quietly suffering now.

It took me a long time to realize that my husband's addiction was not

Sex Sells

According to UNICEF, girls 13 to 18 years of age constitute the largest group in the sex industry. It is estimated that 500,000 girls below age 18 are victims of trafficking each year.

Pornography is big business, bringing in an estimated $10 billion each year.

The National Council on Sexual Addiction Compulsivity estimates that 6 to 8 percent of Americans are sex addicts. According to the National Coalition Against Pornography (NCAP), most sex addicts come to view sex solely as a vehicle for their own physical pleasure. They come to see it as an act without consequence with a person who doesn't matter, and they view marriage and sound relationships as barriers to happiness. This leads to breakdowns in relationships and often divorce.

my fault. It wasn't because I was too tall, too short, too thin, or not thin enough. It wasn't because my hair was brown, blonde, red, or black. It wasn't because my breasts were too small or too large or my cellulite too visible. It wasn't because of my childhood, family, or job. It was because he was tempted daily, and he chose to give in to it.

Our nation has been assaulted by runaway sex campaigns. If I ruled the world, I'd ask all women to begin informing and teaching our world what it means to respect women. How might women do that, you might wonder. Don't let men use you as objects. Help them understand the difference between loving you and lusting for you. Stop getting plastic surgery to prove your worth. Know who you are, appreciate what you've been created to do, and embrace it. Don't make purchases from companies that use advertisements that exploit women. Turn off your TV. Cancel the magazine subscriptions that bring pornography to your home.

We are a very powerful gender. Unfortunately, we have not fully understood how to use that power. If we come together and work to shift our societal behaviors on sex, if we as women embrace ourselves exactly as we are and begin to express our sexuality on our terms instead of those of the images showered upon us, we may begin to create the changes necessary to combat pornography.

SHERI BURR, 40, is a single mom with three daughters. She is a former Las Vegas cocktail waitress who now oversees a divorce recovery group for adults and children.

We'd Respect Alternative Healing Therapies

People are beginning to resist the rhythm of the machine and suspect that the path of inner harmony and health demands an inward attention.

—Gay Gaer Luce, writer and researcher

When I was pregnant and planning a home birth, my midwife spent an hour with me at each appointment, answered all of my questions, and provided research on all of the tests and procedures so that I could make up my own mind. She's an OB nurse as well, and blends alternative and Western medical approaches beautifully. She encouraged me to get acupuncture treatments to help speed my labor, and when my baby's position kept me from progressing, she suggested a second treatment. After the needles came out, I started pushing within half an hour!

Besides being a mother of two, I'm a craniosacral therapist working in an alternative health clinic specializing in women's and children's health.

What Is a Doula?

A *doula* provides emotional and physical support to women in labor and their partners. Although doulas are not medical professionals, their services range from coping techniques to massages and aromatherapy. Research shows that doulas reduce Caesareans by 50 percent, report a shorter labor by 25 percent, and decrease epidural requests by 60 percent. For more information, visit www.dona.org.

Alternative Medicine is Becoming More Mainstream

Established by Congress in 1998, the National Council for Complementary and Alternative Medicine (nccam.nih.gov) is dedicated to exploring and teaching complementary and alternative healing practices and disseminating authoritative information to the public and professionals.

One patient recently told me she had described my treatments to her doctor, and the doctor told her that it all sounded good and to keep seeing me. I was impressed, until I told my friend the acupuncturist this story. She laughed and said, "Sure, they'll endorse you when they can't do anything themselves."

If women ruled the world, complementary therapy would be the first recommendation out of a doctor's mouth. Doctors would feel buoyed by our successes rather than threatened by them. Insurance would always cover complementary therapies, recognizing that a few alternative treatments might prevent a costly and painful surgery, improve people's lives, and cut down on sick days.

Jaala Spiro wants *you* to vote! She lives in Wisconsin with her lively kids and lovely husband, writing and knitting between work and trips to the park and the library.

Call to Action

Question Conventional Medicine

- Research alternative healing therapies. A good place to start is www.amfoundation.org.
- Question your doctor; ask for a thorough explanation of your condition, where you can find research on whatever you're diagnosed with, and, if tests are required, an explanation of what each test is for and what different results might mean.

We Would All Have Health Care

There is no question in my mind but that rights are never won unless people are willing to fight for them.

—Eleanor Smeal, president of Feminist Majority

For me, living without health care has become just another part of my life. I no longer wake up in the morning and think, "Please don't let any of us get sick today," but I do still think of a doctor's visit as an unthinkable luxury, only for emergencies. In the year that we've been without insurance, we've been very lucky and have only had to pay for routine visits to pediatricians and general practitioners, no specialists needed. I no longer have nightmares of broken bones, piles of hospital bills, whispers in my ears of "foreclosure" and "bankruptcy" when I awake. But then something will remind me, such as the receptionist asking if our "status" has changed, and I have to shake my head "No," or I have to explain to someone yet again that my two jobs, combined with my husband's temporary work, adds up to just enough to make us not technically poor, and yet none of these part-time jobs come with insurance that costs less than $900 a month for a family of four.

Our Priorties

Basic health care and nutrition would cost $13 billion for the world. In Europe and the United States, it is estimated that $17 billion a year is spent on pet food and $21 billion a year is spent on cosmetics and perfumes.

It is inconceivable to me that there are so many people like us, who are working incredibly hard and yet lack basic necessities of life. It is incomprehensible that businesses are allowed to have the majority of their workforce be part time, or contractual, or temporary, or whatever euphemistic term they choose for a job with no benefits. One of my jobs requires a master's degree, the other not even a high school diploma, but neither offers a retirement plan, sick days, or health insurance.

For a country as proud of itself as we are, as insistent that we are the world's superpower, what kind of security do we offer our citizens? How can we expect to have a healthy, educated, optimistic population if we make no real efforts in that direction? Why are there still women and children dying city blocks away from the greatest medical institutions in the world? There are countries in this world where every citizen is insured, from birth to death. How amazing it must be to take that for granted, to have that security, no matter who your parents are or what job you have. Yet even in these countries, many noncitizens are denied health care by virtue of their place of birth, as if they are somehow less deserving. Who decides who gets to live or die?

I trust female leadership would begin to solve this problem. Women are generally the ones who see and suffer from the ravages caused by a lack of health care. We are the ones caring for elderly relatives who can no longer afford their prescriptions. We are the ones hoping the childhood fevers don't turn into coughs, which can turn into colds, which can turn into pneumonia we can't afford to have diagnosed, much less treated. We are the ones with unnoticed limps, sprains that never healed, teeth that ache off and on for years, back problems exacerbated by the pink- and blue-collar jobs that require hours on our feet. We are the ones who watch our partners leave the house each day and come home with mysterious bruises, trouble breathing, and missing fingertips.

Health care should be a gift to each citizen of the world and should not stop or start with a paycheck. No mother should have to worry as I do about keeping her family healthy and safe.

JACKIE REGALES lives and teaches in Baltimore, Maryland, with her husband and two daughters. She is 25 years old and enjoys writing, reading, and thinking about revolution.

We'd Get Two Bucks' Value for Every Dollar Spent

What most people don't seem to realize is that there is just as much money to be made out of the wreckage of a civilization as from the upbuilding of one.

—Margaret Mitchell, novelist

Okay, it's probably not accurate to ascribe all virtue to the distaff side of the aisle. The Bush administration boasts its share of estrogen, suggesting there *are* women among us who have no problem with stolen elections, the unilateral invasion of sovereign nations, the use of public monies to bail out multinational corporations that fly the U.S. flag, monopoly market protections for big campaign contributors, the abridgement of civil rights, and the for-profit degradation of our natural environments. Yep, some women are *bad,* and not in a good way. Still, short of Mrs. MacBeth or Caligula's mom, it's hard to imagine a single or a partnered woman who wouldn't spend the family resources to promote the good of the family instead of handing it over to the rich folks who live on the other side of town.

Manipulate the economic indicators any way you want to, but it's getting harder and harder to deny that we're experiencing a prolonged period of national economic angst equaled in recent memory only by the one we call the "great" depression. Our educational institutions are in crisis, failing to provide enough skilled workers to keep our roving corporations home. Health care is so far from being either universal or affordable that I'd move to Canada tomorrow if I were sick. The information age empowers some of us and leaves others alone in the dark. Several million of us have been unemployed so long we've fallen off the newspaper graphics and into the dustbin of despair, no more worthy of notice than the discarded burger wrappers that blow up the street in a stiff wind.

History says it's a disenfranchised middle class that starts revolutions. Franklin D. Roosevelt, they say, saved the ailing patient, capitalism, by the canny application of social welfare remedies. It's time, I say, to spend our money solving our own problems, the way any sensible hausfrau does. Let our unemployed technocrats teach our children and design databases for our nonprofits, show our seniors how to use the Internet, and build networks that promote democracy. Let us wrest health care from the stranglehold of the hospital, the insurance company, and the drug lord and make our living caring for one another, as practical nurses, nutritionists, diagnosticians, hospice workers, aides. Let us refurbish our park system the way our forebears built it, through a new Works Progress Administration.

We should not be spending our national resources to pay mercenaries to fight on foreign soil. Instead, we need to focus on domestic issues, extending our notion of fundamental rights to include upward mobility through uniformly excellent education, health care that is both class- and color-blind, transportation that joins workers and jobs without debasing the environment, financial institutions that support small acts of individual entrepreneurship. We need to fund intensive medical, pharmaceutical, and technical research projects that find the most elegant and least expensive answers, not the ones that can be privately owned and milked for profit. We need to make public investment in local assets and amenities. Only a failure of the imagination shortens the list of ways in which our personal and community lives could be improved by keeping our tax dollars home. No good parent concentrates all family income in the hands of just one favored child. We should be paying each other to solve our common problems and meet our common needs. Every dollar spent that way yields two dollars' worth of value. That's called domestic economy. In big ways and small, women practice it all the time.

What Is The War in Iraq Costing Us?

The Congressional Budget Office estimated the cost to occupy Iraq through 2013 at up to $200 billion, depending on troop levels. Military spending worldwide increased dramatically in 2003, to $956 billion.

Also, according to the United Nations, basic education for every person in the world would cost $6 billion; water and sanitation for everyone in the world would cost $9 billion; and reproductive health care for all women in the world would cost $12 billion.

JOYCE THOMPSON in the author of 10 books, nine of them fiction, and the mother of two kids. Now 55, she lives in Oakland, California, with husband Schuyler Ingle.

We Would Make Heroes of Those Who Demand Peace

It isn't enough to talk about peace.
One must believe in it. And it isn't enough
to believe in it. One must work at it.

—Eleanor Roosevelt, former first lady

How do you raise a boy to know peace in a world that increasingly embraces war? How do you nurture a peacemaker? I wondered that as I watched my sweet little 21-month-old baby boy, Max, sleeping next to me, as only a few miles away, the blast of bombs could be heard from military exercises at a nearby testing range.

As Max lay there beside me lost in baby-boy dreams, his long eyelashes brushing against soft pink cheeks, the house began to reverberate from the blasts going on just a few miles to the north of our San Marcos, California, home. Marines at Camp Pendleton were once again learning the fine art of war, and according to the local news, the blasts would continue throughout the week in preparation of the war to come.

It was not something new, these tests, but with recent events something that I had usually laughed off as "little boys playing war games" now took on a much more serious tone. The images of bloody bodies on the news weren't the result of a game.

Outside, I could hear the shouts of neighborhood children playing basketball, and adults chattering around the mailboxes, catching up on the latest gossip. It was the picture of normalcy, a friendly cul-de-sac where just about everybody knew each other by name. Every now and then, another bomb went off, an unpleasant reminder that amidst that happy illusion, the war was never too far off, hovering on the perimeters like a potential pedophile standing outside an elementary school gate.

As I snuggled up against Max, I wondered how it was possible that someone so small and needy and adorable could grow up one day to go off and kill other human beings, all in the name of "country" or "patriotism" or, worst of all, "God." He was a blank canvas, and I knew in my heart that I would be only one of many artists who would try to imprint my vision upon him before he reached manhood.

I know that there are people who want to kill and make war and commit acts of violence for monetary gain or nationalistic pride or religious fanaticism or just plain power. But I believe that peace is *always* a better choice than war. If women ruled the world, we would honor those who fight for peace the same way we honor those who go off to make war. Rarely does the news media focus on the peacemakers. Shockingly, they are viewed as loonies, peaceniks, rainbow-clad and long-haired hippies. But really the peace lovers are you and me, mothers and fathers and children.

She Stood Alone

On September 15, 2001, a resolution authorizing Bush to use "all necessary and appropriate force" against anyone associated with the terrorist attacks of September 11 passed 98–0 in the Senate and 420–1 in the House. California Representative Barbara Lee, the only dissenting vote, stated on the floor, "There must be some of us who say, 'Let's step back for a moment and think through the implications of our actions today—let us more fully understand the consequences.'"

As a mother, I am committed to raising Max as a peacemaker who loves and respects others—I will try to teach him by my own example, by showing him how choices can be made from the heart and the spirit. I will help him to look at every side of a situation, to gain a better understanding of it before he makes a choice, so that when he does, he does so from a position of intelligence and empowerment. Most of all, I will try to instill in him a positive vision of the universe as a friendly place, and encourage him to respond to life accordingly. I know that the world will try to make him cynical, harsh, hostile, powerless and prejudiced, and that politicians, the media, and many of his peers will strive to keep him "one of the crowd," because true leadership is often threatening to the status quo—especially when the status quo is one based upon war, aggression, and greed.

My hope is that he will realize he always has the final choice: to go along blindly, or to be authentic to the inner voice deep within himself. Then maybe, just maybe, Max will grow up to know exactly what he can do to make the world a better place.

He will spread peace.

REV. MARIE D. JONES is a New Thought minister and author of the award-winning book *Looking for God in All the Wrong Places.* She is 42, married, and has one toddler son, Max.

Nonviolence Resources

Web Sites

Fellowship for Reconciliation (www.forusa.org)

METTA Center for Nonviolence Education (www.mettacenter.org)

Nonviolence International (www.nonviolenceinternational.net)

Books

The Search for a Nonviolent Future by Michael N. Nagler

Nonviolent Communication by Marshall B. Rosenberg, Ph.D.

"American Women": A Poem for the Struggle for Equality

Coming together,
Hand in hand.
The circle of support.

My sister overseas
I know your anger
When you are forced
into sterilization or to abort
Because a girl was to be born.

The calamity caused by speaking freely.
If you choose to, death is cast upon you.

The shackles of arranged marriages
Scar your ankles and your children.

Enforced gender roles spare no female.
Illiteracy to keep your daughters
and yourselves enslaved and subservient.

Quiet, unheard and maimed.

The stones that strike your cloaked face,
If you dare to cause one another to think.

The sexual genitalia mutilation performed to rob and
reiterate
Your female identity.

The Ceremony of Cremation of Living Widows
Is an act of society, showing you your place.
If your husband dies, so must you.
The final price your purchase brings.

Your struggles aren't so un-American.
In fact our stories are very alike.

American Women jest at times,
quite ignorantly,
of our "new" found liberty.

Let us not forget our equality is yet amended,
And our progress not yet done nor universal.
Nor is our struggle at home or abroad,
against oppression eclipsed.

Davina Rhine is a 27-year-old tattooed vegetarian mommy living in Texas with her husband, Jason, and son, Corben. Currently she is writing *The Mommy Manifesto,* which she hopes will fuel change for women and children globally.

The Compassion to Embrace the World

Section 6

This is a time in history when women's voices must be heard, or forever be silenced. It's not because we think we are better than men, but we think differently. It's not women against men, but women and men. It's not that the world would have been better if women had run it, but that the world will be better when we as women, who bring our own perspective, share in running it.

—Betty Bumpers, political figure and activist

Introduction

We Would All Have a Say

Kavita Nandini Ramdas, president and CEO, the Global Fund for Women

From the time I was a young girl in India, I understood that having daughters was considered to be a huge misfortune. Even educated middle-class family friends would think nothing of telling my mother, "Oh what a shame, you only have three daughters." My parents always responded by saying that they considered their three daughters to be nothing but good fortune. My parents encouraged us to think for ourselves, to value diversity and debate, and to believe that our opinions mattered, and we in turn believed that we could make valuable contributions to the world.

Yet, millions of girls around the world are born into conditions that silence them and prevent them from contributing to society. In almost all societies, women and girls face deep-rooted and systemic discrimination that significantly restricts their freedom and inhibits them from realizing their full potential.

Yet we know and can prove that what is good for women is good for the world. Important changes happen when women's voices are heard. The success of the Ugandan ABC (Abstinence, Be faithful, and use a

Condom) campaign demonstrates this so well. This pioneering campaign has resulted in an impressive decrease in the rates of infection of AIDS/HIV among the general population in Uganda. The Ugandan women were actively supported by their government when they used the strategy of abstinence as a negotiating tool with male partners whose infidelity put them at constant risk of sexually transmitted disease. Ugandan women's organizations encouraged their members to refuse to have sex with husbands and partners who were known to have multiple partners or wives in other villages or simply a roving eye. This was not some kind of moralistic or puritanical decree but rather an incredibly powerful act of collective action for lasting social change. At the same time, there was a countrywide mass sex education campaign spearheaded by grassroots women's organizations that encouraged youth, women, and men to speak honestly and frankly about issues of sex, power, and sexual behavior.

The Ugandan story found echoes in the recent efforts of the global peace movement that sought to prevent a war in Iraq. Women peace activists around the globe performed the ancient Greek play *Lysistrata,* which tells the tale of women who withheld sex from men until they found peaceful means to end war.

When women are part of making decisions and coming up with solutions to the problems that they face, we all benefit. Women in Indonesia have purchased their own radio station so that they can share strategies for achieving gender equality; women in Colombia have organized massive peace rallies to pressure the government to end the pervasive violence; and women in Afghanistan continue to lead a national movement to rebuild schools, train teachers, and provide income-generating opportunities for young people, both girls and boys.

In a sense, women around the world have been given a special gift—we know firsthand what it means to be denied power and participation. This understanding allows us to envision another world in which women and men can live without fear and participate equally in all aspects of society.

KAVITA NANDINI RAMDAS is president and chief executive officer of the Global Fund for Women. Kavita is recognized as a leader in the fields of women's rights and philanthropy.

MOTHER'S DAY PROCLAMATION, 1870

Arise then . . . women of this day!
Arise, all women who have hearts!
Whether your baptism be of water or of tears!
Say firmly:
"We will not have questions answered by irrelevant agencies,
Our husbands will not come to us, reeking with carnage,
For caresses and applause.
Our sons shall not be taken from us to unlearn
All that we have been able to teach them of charity, mercy and patience.
We, the women of one country,
Will be too tender of those of another country
To allow our sons to be trained to injure theirs."

From the voice of a devastated Earth a voice goes up with
Our own. It says: "Disarm! Disarm!
The sword of murder is not the balance of justice."
Blood does not wipe our dishonor,
Nor violence indicate possession.
As men have often forsaken the plough and the anvil
At the summons of war,
Let women now leave all that may be left of home
For a great and earnest day of counsel.
Let them meet first, as women, to bewail and commemorate the dead.
Let them solemnly take counsel with each other as to the means
Whereby the great human family can live in peace . . .
Each bearing after his own time the sacred impress, not of Caesar,
But of God—
In the name of womanhood and humanity, I earnestly ask
That a general congress of women without limit of nationality,
May be appointed and held at someplace deemed most convenient
And the earliest period consistent with its objects,
To promote the alliance of the different nationalities,
The amicable settlement of international questions,
The great and general interests of peace.

JULIA WARD HOWE was a reformer, writer, and poet. Active in the women's rights movement, she played a prominent role in several suffrage organizations and in women's clubs. She is best known as the writer of "The Battle Hymn of the Republic."

No Woman Would Die of an Illegal Abortion

If we value women as worthy of the protection of fundamental rights, we must value their power not to be forced to bear a child for another's purpose.

—Faye Wattleton, former president of Planned Parenthood

When a young woman entered menarche, older women who love her, including her mother, would gather around and say,

"You in your now fertile woman's body, you have been given a great opportunity and a great responsibility. You have within you the ability to nurture life; within you a zygote can become an embryo; an embryo can become a fetus, and a fetus can become a beloved child. But do not rush to experience this miracle of birth. First, discover who you are."

Then each young woman entering menarche would be presented with her very own speculum. Instructed on how to use it, she would gather her mirror and her flashlight and retreat to a quiet place, to examine her cervix. And having seen her cervix, the young woman would be determined never to let anyone else control it.

She would be presented with a magnificent dinner, with eggplant and fresh-baked bread, and the wise women would say, "For right now, we are all safe. But each time a young woman enters menarche we must remember that there was a time when the desire to control teenage girl's sexuality dominated the world, when distrust of women's ability to make life and death decisions sentenced many women to death."

The March for Women's Lives

1,150,000 people march on Washington, D.C., April 25, 2004, to voice opposition to government attacks on women's reproductive rights and health:

"My friends—make no mistake. There is a war on choice. We didn't start it, but we are going to win it! They're not just after abortion rights. This is a full-throttle war on your very health—on your access to real sex education, birth control, medical privacy, and life-saving research."

—Gloria Feldt, president of Planned Parenthood Federation of America

"My greatest wish is that there would never be another political debate about the right to choose. But history teaches us that every right—no matter how basic—is always at risk. And I'm confident that the young people who have led this march today will lead our movement in a new wave of activism that will keep the right to choose alive for the next generation."

—Kate Michelman, president of NARAL Pro-Choice America

"This march is a giant wake-up call. We won't go back to 1968, when women couldn't buy birth control; we won't go back to 1972, when women were dying from illegal abortions. We're marching for our rights before it's too late."

—Kim Gandy, president of the National Organization for Women (NOW)

And then, together, they would remember and recount the past:

"Women have always known how to end pregnancies. We remember the women killed as witches who possessed the knowledge of pregnancy-ending herbs. We remember enslaved women who knew how to keep slave owners from profiting from rape. We remember the Jane Collective, who learned how to perform abortions. We remember doctors who were murdered, nurses who were attacked, volunteers who risked their safety, to help women end unwanted pregnancies. We remember a time when women's bodies were used as campaign fodder, selling us out piece by piece, choice by choice, right by right."

The wise women would dance around the young woman and pledge to teach her to honor and control her own fertility. Finally, one older woman, a trusted and beloved friend, would step forward and say, "You in your fertile woman's body, you have been given a great opportunity and a great responsibility. We love you and we trust you. If you need us, we are nearby, for you need never be alone."

CAROL J. ADAMS is the author of *The Sexual Politics of Meat, The Pornography of Meat, Woman-Battering, Prayers for Animals and Animal Lovers,* and several other books and edited collections. She has been a pro-choice activist since the early 1970s.

Baby Girls Would Always Be Cause to Celebrate

What its children become, that will the community become.

—Suzanne LaFollette, politician and writer

The year is 1960. The place is a small village in southern Italy. It is springtime, and a baby is trying to be born. There is only one attending midwife at the small house. The fetus has been stuck in the birth canal for two days, and the mother, who is only 20 years old, seems to be slipping in and out of consciousness.

When the doctor finally arrives, he tells everyone that the baby is probably dead and that it's best to focus on saving the mother's life. The father of the baby is stunned. This is their first child. In absolute denial, he reaches inside his wife's body expecting a miracle, and he receives it.

A fetus's arms are normally tucked into the body, making it easy for the head to emerge first through the birth canal. Not in this case. This fetus has outstretched arms, making it nearly impossible for it to be born. But when the father's hand comes near, the tiny hands wrap themselves around the man's finger. The man is delirious with excitement. He begins shouting and hugging his wife. "The baby is alive. The baby is alive!" The woman, renewed by her husband's encouragement, gives it one last attempt, and a baby girl emerges into the world.

The mother takes one look at her newborn baby and under a tearful breath says, "I did all that; I nearly died, and it's not even a boy?"

That baby girl was me. My mother came from a culture that celebrated the masculine and denigrated the feminine. Baby boys were wanted. Baby girls were a burden. I knew about my mother's rejection at my birth my whole life, but it didn't produce strong feelings until after I had given birth to my own firstborn (a boy), 30 years later. It was then that my outrage was activated. How could she reject me because I was girl?! It took several months of working through the hurt and the anger before my compassion was able to understand her point of view. My mother had been conditioned to hate her gender, so when she had me she felt as if she had failed. My mother was the victim of so much unfairness. Her brother got to go to school while she had to stay home to take care of her handicapped sister.

My birth story, told to me by my grandmother, was a driving force throughout my life. I have fought against stereotypes and broken the mold. I left home at 18 to live alone in Paris, France. I lived with my now-husband before getting married. I had both my parents walk me down the aisle. I kept my own name. I even gave one of our children my last name. I broke the rules for women in my culture, and today I help other women take the step toward empowerment and freedom.

If women ruled the world, baby girls born anywhere on this planet would be a cause for celebration. There would be fireworks and balloons, champagne and flowers, and many, many joyful smiles. Family and friends and the community at large would feel blessed that another little girl had been sent to them.

Grace Cirocco, 44, is the author of the Canadian best-seller *Take the Step, the Bridge Will be There.* A leading authority on women's leadership and wellness, Grace delivers keynote presentations and runs transformational retreats for women.

The Growing Trend of More Boys than Girls

United Press International reported that in 2002, for every 100 newborn girls, there were 117 boys born in China. If this trend continues, China will have up to 40 million more men than women by 2020. Due to this national crisis, the government has designated 2004 as the year to promote sexual equality.

Data from India's 2001 census shows that the sex ratio for 0-6 year olds fell from 945 females per 1,000 males in 1991 to 927 per 1,000 in 2001. Compare this with the world average of 1,050 females to 1,000 males.

Female Genital Mutilation Would Cease to Exist

If you are trying to transform a brutalized society into one where people can live in dignity and hope, you begin with the empowering of the most powerless. You build from the ground up.

—Adrienne Rich, poet, educator, and activist

If women ruled the world, female genital mutilation (FGM) would be as foreign today as microchips would have been in prehistoric times. It simply would not exist, in fact, because women would not create ritualistic practices nor condone the hacking of their bodies in order to unconditionally prove their chastity, worth, or purity or because they believed their sex impure and dirty.

As an American mother of color who has birthed two daughters of my own, imagining the horrific reality of FGM and even trying to comprehend its "necessary" place in many indigenous cultures proves far too difficult. Yet the fact remains that more than two million girls of color are at risk of circumcision each year, based on recent estimates by the World Health Organization. Sadly, these numbers do not seem to be waning significantly enough for us to declare even a partial victory over this cultural blight, despite the rigorous efforts of international health and women's organizations to eradicate FGM.

According to Amnesty International, FGM is practiced in more than 28 African countries; some Middle Eastern countries, such as Oman and

Yemen; and a few Asian countries where there is a significant Muslim population, such as Indonesia, Sri Lanka, and Malaysia. Western nations with large immigrant populations, such as Denmark, France, Italy, Britain, and even the United States, report that FGM is taking place inside of their borders, bringing old-world customs head to head with industrialized cultures that stand clearly against the practice of female circumcision. These Western countries are working hard to ensure that young girls do not undergo FGM by educating women and men about the severity of the health implications that result and also by informing them that FGM is a cultural practice, although deep-rooted, and not one based on religious doctrine.

Protesting FGM

Equality Now has created the Women's Action Network to protest human rights violations, including FGM, against women and girls around the world (www.equalitynow.org).

Because I am an active advocate of issues that affect women of color, FGM touches a sensitive chord with me. By either performing FGM on small girls or allowing it to take place, mothers, in effect, abort their inherent right to protect their daughters and at the same time strip young girls from having a say over their own bodies and biology. FGM, therefore, brings to the fore not only issues of human rights but also those of women's rights. Most importantly, however, FGM highlights the lack of mothers' rights in the countries where FGM exists. I believe that all mothers should have the right to protect their children without regard to traditional practices. One step in this direction would be to help mothers make informed decisions against FGM and empower them to take a strong stand against sexism.

Older women, those primarily entrusted to perform FGM on girls, must also take a stand against FGM. These women are often the purveyors of the ageless cultural demand of subservience and subordination. With every slit and cut, with every thorn that is pushed into place, and with the endless, senseless agony that the girls feel, these older women are further reminders that women do not rule. Women are not the rulers. Women are ruled. And to further prove their inequality, women themselves help to keep the sexist traditions alive by believing in these practices' inherent good and their traditional worth.

If women ruled the world, the countryside and villages the world over would be safe places to live and grow for girls and women, not the brutal cesspools of traditional ceremonies that are still practiced religiously and without let-up.

If women ruled, female genital mutilation wouldn't have a place in this anthology. It wouldn't exist and thus would need no space for discussion. Only, though, if women ruled.

JENNIFER JAMES, 29, is the publisher of *Mommy Too!* (www.mommytoo.com), an online magazine for mothers of color, as well as the director of the National African-American Homeschoolers Alliance.

We Would Walk a Mile in Each Other's Shoes

em·pa·thy n.: *direct identification with, understanding of, and vicarious experience of another person's situation, feelings, and motives*

When we can understand or relate to the experiences of others, we are less inclined to do those things that cause suffering to them and more inclined to support those things that allow for joy. In order for men to experience more empathy with the powerlessness and pain, as well as the joy, of being female, we would turn the tables on all the men if we ruled the world. And, men would, for a finite amount of time, get a taste of their own behavior and also experience some of the wonderfulness of being a woman.

Men would be much less desired by society than women and would be taught from a young age that their goal in life is to please and serve women. Men would be considered less intelligent than women by teachers and other people in authority. They would be made to feel awkward in their bodies and only attractive if they twisted and contorted themselves into uncomfortable clothing and high-heeled shoes. They would need to flirt and pander to the power women in their communities and workplaces in order to get ahead, and they'd have to work much harder, for longer hours, and be paid less than women for doing the same job. Men would be expected to give sexual favors to the women they were trying to impress; they would worry about their financial futures while women could sit pretty on their IRAs and generous retirement policies. Men would be seen as "over the hill" once they turned 30, while women would be seen as becoming better and better, more and more attractive, as they got older.

Men would be made to defer to women's decisions about everything important. They would stay home and take care of the babies and young children while women went out into society to work and plan and engage in developing their minds. Men would have to wear head covering to protect their modesty; have dowries and be married off in their teens. Men would have the first half of their penises cut off when they attained preadolescence so their sexual urges, and desire to be sexual, would be curtailed.

International Inequities

Around the world women today still don't have basic rights:

Saudi Arabia: Women are segregated in public places; they cannot drive cars; they must be covered from head to toe in public; they cannot be admitted to a hospital without their husbands' permission.

Jordan: Women can only drive if their faces are covered. Marital rape is legal; wife-beating is rampant, and often allowed by law; and honor killings receive minimal sentences. Such honor killings have become so common that they comprised 25 percent of the total murders committed in Jordan in 2000.

Men would also get to experience the wonders of feeling life grow inside of them and giving birth to another human being. Men would know what it's like to have the comfort of a community of males with whom they could be truly vulnerable and with whom they could talk, not just about sports and how to fix things, but also about their anxieties and worries and hopes and dreams. Men would be able to get hugs and gentleness from other men without feeling weak or less manly for it. Men would be able to cry and show fear without being ridiculed or humiliated because of their sex. Men would be able to change their minds and change their jobs and have the choice to stay home with the kids or go out to work without seeming less manly for their decision. Men would know what it's like to be emotionally connected to both men and women in deep and meaningful ways.

After feeling the inadequacies, misfortunes, and joys of this state of affairs, we women would then let the men off the hook. After having this experience, men would see the world differently, and, together, women and men would create a different, more equitable and nurturing world.

We would promote programs and policies that allow all children to grow up feeling confident and strong: child care, health care, medical care, elder care, and education would be our first priorities. We would put people before profits and dismantle all weapons of mass destruction. We would outlaw all wars and instead create educational policies that teach emotional literacy and relationship skills. We would teach people how to mediate conflict and how to be accepting of differences.

We would learn how to better share what we have and protect the world's resources. We would develop the arts and music, as well as policies and programs that would help sustain a green and healthy planet. We would create advertisements that made people feel good about themselves instead of bad.

We would encourage and support peace. We would develop a culture of community and spiritual growth. Finally, we would discourage materialism and selfishness and individualistic success at the expense of others and our environments.

MARY MENG-LIANG NI is a 55-year-old first-generation Chinese American, mother, stepmother, widow, teacher, squash player, procrastinator, dog owner, pursuer of truth and justice. She's lived in a cooperative housing group with 12 other families in Boston, Massachusetts, for the past 25 years.

~ Something to Think About ~

WOULD WE BE FAIR AND JUST?

Women, with their motherly instincts—born to protect, to comfort, to heal, to seek what is right and just—would not start a war without provocation; they would not want young people to die simply to satisfy their egos. Or would they? Cleopatra and Lucrezia Borgia were powerful women, but did the world become a better place because of them? Would women be more compassionate with the weak and suffering, would they be able to help the abused and the poor? Once they were in positions of power, would they keep their integrity and high intentions or could they be corrupted by money and power just as men who rule?

—Elfriede Wegener, 76

We'd Develop a Blueprint for Peace

The struggle to maintain peace is immeasurably more difficult than any military operation.

—Anne O'Hare McCormick, journalist

Today, more than ever, we need to join the peace movement to protect the world we are living in and join with our sisters around the world to protect the future of all Earth's children and other threatened species.

I often wonder if the average woman with a baby on her hip knows that the Project for the New American Century, entitled "Rebuilding America's Defenses: Strategies, Forces and Resources for a New Century" has great plans for our children now gurgling at our breasts. This massive "rebuilding" campaign, run under the guise of "space exploration," intends to control and own space. Do mothers know that their cherished offspring might inherit the future mammoth task of arming the heavens? All the information is out there, but we are so busy nurturing our families and living our lives—who has time to research this future space plan manifesto! Let me break it down for you.

The Air Force Space Command Strategic Master Plan outlines the United States' intention to dominate the world by turning space into a 21 century battlefield. This document details how our government is developing high-tech weapons, nuclear warheads, and spacecraft that will enable the United States to hit any target on Earth within seconds.

It also boastfully states that any other power with even a toehold in space is intolerable. The United States wants to *own* space—surely this is reason enough for women to take their rightful seats at the table of global consequence.

The peace movement needs a blueprint for action to counter the blueprint for U.S. global domination that is now being formulated. And it needs to be acted upon immediately!

The global peace movement is capable of drawing up a workable plan for the preservation and sanctity of all life on Earth. We have peace troops on the ground everywhere! We could start the Project for the Survival of Earth (PSE) and work on biodiversity conservation, protecting our environment, and creating a better world for our children. The PSE would focus on dismantling armaments, outlawing munitions sales globally, and advocating negotiation instead of war.

Helen Caldicott is recognized globally for peace advocacy. She founded Physicians for Social Responsibility and the Women's Action for Nuclear Disarmament (WAND). In association with physicians and scientists, Dr. Caldicott plays a major role in educating the people of New Zealand and Australia about the vast dangers of nuclear production and development. We could extend this to the rest of the world.

Vadnana Shiva is working right now on biodiversity conservation, food security, globalization, economic liberalization, patenting and intellectual property rights, biopiracy, biotechnology, biosafety, toxics and hazardous wasters, aquaculture, plant breeders' rights and farmers' rights over their seed, sustainable agriculture, the World Trade Organization, and GATT (General Agreement on Tariffs and Trade). That is way too much for one person! She says, "Today the world is on the brink of a biological diversity crisis. The constantly diminishing store of biodiversity on our planet poses an enormous environmental threat—of which far too few people are aware." Caldicott and Shiva are only two examples of great female minds able to conceive a worldview of what is needed for Project for the Survival of Earth to be successful.

Splinter groups with similar Earth stewardship philosophies could merge globally and then again with Project for the Survival of Earth. PSE could then integrate its finances to counter military spending and redirect it to more humanitarian causes like nonpropagandized education and national health care.

Why leave everything up to one famous man or woman to step forward when we the people have the right to speak up in a democracy and make steps toward peace and tranquility, away from war and chaos. We, the masses, have the power to stop making enemies faster than we can kill them. Let us take our inspiration from a collective vision. Let's take peace into our own hands now.

Colonizing Space

In November 2000, 138 nations voted in the United Nations to reaffirm the Outer Space Treaty, stating specifically that space be set aside "for peaceful purposes." Only the United States and Israel abstained, and U.S. plans for "Full Spectrum dominance" continue to move forward.

JANE EVERSHED has been painting socially conscious art for more than 20 years. She is also a mother, speaker, poet, writer, art teacher, and activist who currently sits on the board of Women Against Military Madness (www.worldwidewamm.org).

Female Nobel Peace Prize Winners

1905 **Bertha von Suttner** from Austria won for her pacifist novel *Die Waffen nieder* (1889, tr. *Lay Down Your Arms,* 1892).

1931 **Jane Addams** was a leader in the woman's suffrage and pacifist movements in the United States.

1947 **Emily G. Balch** was the cofounder of the Women's International League for Peace and Freedom with Jane Addams.

1976 **Mairead Corrigan** and **Betty Williams** formed the Peace People Organization, a movement of Catholics and Protestants dedicated to ending sectarian fighting in Northern Ireland.

1979 **Mother Teresa of Calcutta** founded the Missionaries of Charity.

1982 **Alva Myrdal** of Sweden won for her work in the nuclear disarmament movement.

1991 **Daw Aung San Suu Kyi** led the National League for Democracy (NLD) and won the Nobel Peace Prize for her nonviolent struggles against the military leaders of Myanmar.

1992 **Rigoberta Menchú** has worked to secure and protect the rights of indigenous peoples in Guatemala and to promote intercultural peace.

1997 **Jody Williams** of the United States won for her work for the International Campaign to Ban Landmines.

2003 **Shirin Ebadi** was honored for her efforts for democracy and human rights and her outspoken struggle to change Iran's attitudes toward the rights of women and children.

Call to Action

Help Our Environment

- Join a specific campaign to put pressure on politicians and offending companies. Check out Greenpeace (www.greenpeace.org), the Rainforest Action Network (www.ran.org) , Friends of the Earth (www.foe.org), the Sierra Club (www.sierraclub.org), or the Worldwatch Institute (www.worldwatch.org).
- Avoid supporting companies known to pollute the environment.
- Find uses for items you might normally throw away.
- Support research for alternative and renewable energy sources.
- Vote for politicians and support business leaders who want to restore and preserve our natural resources.
- Support businesses that are finding creative solutions for our waste products or are using recycled materials.
- Practice responsible citizenry in your own home: recycle, save energy, leave a light "footprint."

Earth Rebirth

How do you end a worldwide war
Without the cost of lives?
How do you end a worldwide war
That's always being justified?

If the earth is a functioning biosystem
Of the highest delicacy,
Then why do we allow the ecoterrorists
Such liberty?
They fly fighter jets into the face
Of the very god
They seek to worship and perpetuate.

If man can destroy all of humanity
Then women must see to it
That we no longer continue it,
At the very least, put it on hold,
For this is our ace card
On the stage of world decision
With our sisters from all nations,
There is so little recognition left
For the sanctity of creation.

Patriarchy's rampant endorsement
Of the proliferation of the human species
As superior to all other life forms
Signs its own death warrant,
Disregard for the female populace worldwide
As an integral part of shaping earth's destiny
Abandons the laws of nature itself.
And nature is our origin.
Women need to take their seats
At the table of global consequence,
And rebirth this earth.
Our wombs are our artillery now.

JANE EVERSHED has been painting socially conscious art for more than 20 years. She is also a mother, speaker, poet, writer, art teacher, and activist who currently sits on the board of Women Against Mititary Madness (www.worldwidewamm.org).

There Would Be No Laws That Discriminate Against Women and Girls

There is always time to make right what is wrong.

—Susan Griffin, writer

Since the inception of the United Nations, governments have affirmed the fundamental right to equality in international treaties as well as in national constitutions around the world. Nevertheless, the most blatant forms of state-sanctioned sex discrimination continue virtually everywhere. Often under the guise of religion, tradition, or custom, governments condone and enforce discriminatory laws that perpetuate the unequal economic, marital, and social status of women. In 1995, at the UN Fourth World Conference on Women in Beijing, member states promised to promote equality and the inherent dignity of men and women—yet they still exhibit little or no political will to execute these commitments. Equality Now launched a campaign calling on governments to fulfill their pledge to eradicate sex-discriminatory laws by 2005. That date is fast approaching, and much work needs to be accomplished.

For instance, by law in India and elsewhere, a woman cannot claim she was raped by her husband; in countries as diverse as Japan, Colombia, Romania, and Tanzania, men are not eligible for marriage before 18, but girl children can be married. In Algeria, among other places, a wife must obey her husband and recognize him as head of the family; in Saudi

Arabia, no woman can drive, nor can she vote in Kuwait. In the Philippines, selling sex is a crime, while buying sex is not, thereby criminalizing those who are exploited, mainly women, while exempting those who exploit them, mostly men. In Pakistan and other nations that judge under *sharia* law, a woman's word is worth half of a man's in a court of law, and in Israel, unlike a man, a Jewish woman has no right to divorce, as governed by rabbinical law.

These are only a few examples of pervasive discrimination by law. Even in countries that proudly claim to have no discriminatory laws, the application of laws can have unequal impact on women, such as in the United States, where laws that promote equality in employment rarely guarantee equal pay for work of comparable value, and women continue to be underpaid in sex-segregated jobs.

How do these laws affect women's lives? Ask Woineshet Zebene Negash, a young woman in Ethiopia, who in 2001, at the age of 13, was abducted and raped by Aberew Jemma Negussie. In some regions of Ethiopia, abduction is an old cultural practice used to take a girl as wife by force. Woineshet's rapist was arrested; however, released on bail, he abducted her again with the help of accomplices and held her captive for more than a month until she managed to escape, but only after he had forced her to sign a marriage certificate. Under Ethiopian law, as well as in some other countries around the world, if a rapist marries his victim, he is exempt from criminal responsibility for the rape. Equality Now, in conjunction with the Ethiopian Women's Lawyers Association in Addis Ababa, initiated an international campaign to bring justice to Woineshet and demand that the Ethiopian government abolish its law on rape and abduction. In July 2003, Aberew Jemma Negussie was sentenced to 10 years' imprisonment without parole for the abduction and rape of Woineshet. For the first time in Ethiopia, Negussie's accomplices were also charged and convicted for abduction.

Woineshet's story is one of courage and resistance in the face of seemingly insurmountable obstacles. Her determination to challenge the law is a victory that should embolden people to seek legal redress for all forms of violence and discrimination upheld by governments. Unfortunately, an appellate court overturned the verdict in December 2003, freeing Woineshet's rapist once again. Once again, Equality Now is campaigning for justice. Woineshet will not stop fighting. Her voice echoes those of millions of girls and women, standing up for their rights and calling on us to join them in the struggle for justice and a life free of violence. If women ruled the world, there would be laws to protect and value women's rights, equal to the laws that govern men. State-sanctioned sex discrimination under the guise of religion, tradition, or custom would not exist.

Equality Now

For more information about Woineshet's case and how you can call on the Ethiopian government and other governments to change their discriminatory laws, visit www.equalitynow.org.

TAINA BIEN-AIME is the executive director of Equality Now, an international human rights organization working for the fundamental rights of girls and women.

We'd Banish *All* Fundamentalism

Religion supports and perpetuates
the social organization it reflects.
—Riane Eisler, anthropologist, philosopher, and writer

After September 11, 2001, I began to learn more about the lives of Afghan women under the brutal rule of the Taliban. When I first found the Web site of the Revolutionary Association of the Women of Afghanistan (www.rawa.org), their home page said, "Welcome to the website of the most oppressed women on Earth!" I have learned so much from RAWA's members, who I now know are really the *bravest* women on Earth! They have risked their lives to educate children in democratic values and to strive for human rights for all Afghans. Their Web site now says, "If you are anti-fundamentalist and freedom-loving, you are with us!"

It doesn't matter if they call themselves the Taliban in Afghanistan, the Christian Right in the United States, the Sangh Parivar in India, or hard-line Zionists in Israel, fundamentalists have more in common with each other than with the traditional, peaceful, caring practitioners of the same religion in nonfundamentalist form.

Unable to cope with the enormous questions human beings are facing as the survival of Earth is threatened, fundamentalist men and the women who support them have turned to a rigid set of rules for answers. They have adopted a narrow and literal interpretation of religious scripture, and they seek to impose a rigid set of laws and rules derived from that interpretation on all members of society, even resorting to force and terror to do so. Fundamentalism denies the loving core of every faith, replacing compassion with coercion and tolerance with punishment. Every type of fundamentalism preaches suppression of women and male supremacy. It is a growing danger in many faiths, including Christianity, Islam, Hinduism, and Judaism.

Any person should be free to believe in the literal truth of any text. But when people seek to impose their beliefs on others, they undermine religious freedom and attack other people's right to exist as full human beings.

The fundamentalist imagines that if he can impose his will on everything around him, then he will be saved. The first targets of his confusion, frustration, and aggression are his own mother, wife, and daughters. All of these deadly movements preach loathing for women's bodies and seek to control us, attacking our reproductive rights and imposing codes of dress and behavior.

Everywhere, fundamentalists attempt to deny women basic human rights, such as the right to health care, to education, to earn a livelihood, to choose whether or whom to marry, and whether to bear children. Fundamentalism results in abominations like genital mutilation of girls, forced marriage (even at the age of 9), the selling of women as property, incarceration of women in the home, denial of women's right to vote or to participate as equals in religious practice.

The forced imposition of religious practice is itself the greatest attack on religion, for religion that is backed by terror is robbed of all devotion. Only where there is freedom to worship is worship sincere or meaningful.

In a world where women were empowered, fundamentalism would

Meena

The Revolutionary Association of the Women of Afghanistan (RAWA) fights for human rights and social justice for Afghan women, including programs promoting literacy and income generation (www.rawa.org).

Meena, the founder of RAWA, was a social activist who was organizing and educating Afghan women since 1977. Due to the very effectiveness she had in mobilizing public opinion, she was assassinated for her feminist views in 1987.

be unknown. Mothers would teach their children, both boys and girls, to honor and protect both women and men. The dignity of all persons would be respected, and religious practice, including the wearing of religious symbols and dress, would be a matter of personal choice. Religion would return to its core message of love and reverence for life. Women and men could then turn their energies to preserving and restoring our home on Earth.

MELODY ERMACHILD CHAVIS is the author of *Meena, Heroine of Afghanistan: The Martyr Who Founded RAWA, the Revolutionary Association of the Women of Afghanistan* (St. Martin's Press). She is a grandmother and peace activist.

~ Something to Think About ~

OUR BEST CREATIONS SHOULD LAST WELL BEYOND AGE 18

I believe if women ruled the world, we would all learn from an early age that the job of every human being is to improve the Earth. There would not be wars and bombings of innocent people. Women know what it means when the news says, "Two people were killed in Iraq." They can imagine how the mother felt to have her miracle destroyed. That is what war is, when you think about it: destruction of the millions of miracles women have made.

It takes about 8.25 years of woman's actual physical labor to raise an 18-year-old person. A child takes 100 percent of the mother's time the first two years, 50 percent of her time the next six years, and about 25 percent of her time from ages 9 to 18, for a total of 8.25 years of labor. Multiply 8.25 by the thousands killed in war, and you have billions of years of actual women's labor put to waste in one war. You see, women get that number and shake their heads in disgust. They know the value of those years and the pain of the next 50 years, living with a broken heart.

—Elizabeth McLeod, 11

Feminism Would Not Be a Dirty Word

[Feminism] asks that women be free to define themselves—
instead of having their identity defined for them,
time and again, by their culture and their men.

—Susan Faludi, writer and feminist

"You're not a feminist, are you?" His eyes narrowed suspiciously, his lips curled into a smirk, and he lifted his head with an air of superiority.

It was an average workday—a slow night at the coffee shop—and a conversation with a coworker had just taken an interesting turn as I explained my politics.

It still surprises me that the word *feminist* is seen as such an insult. Strip it down: *Feminism* is defined in my dictionary as "advocacy of increased political activity or rights for women." That sounds great to me! However, like most insults, the word *feminist* gains its negative power from fear. The patriarchy fears it will lose its power to women involved in activism, who threaten entrenched gender roles by speaking out and demanding rights.

In the backlash to feminism of the past three decades, women have been forced to buy into this fear in order to succeed within the patriarchy, hesitating to describe themselves as feminist for fear of appearing too radical. Women who are identified as feminists have been ridiculed, harassed, labeled as lesbians, bitches, the loathsome "feminazis," and worse. A woman might be smart and successful but must stop short of embodying the F-word. By the late '90s, the strength of women and the women's movement had been squelched in the mainstream and reduced to the pop-friendly slogan "girl power." Every day American women enjoy freedoms and rights gained by our foremothers, while too many deny their part in the fight that got us here.

I once saw a bumper sticker that read, "Feminism is the radical notion that women are people." To me, that means we reject the many notions upheld by the patriarchy: That we are decorations or trophies, and our bodies are made to be whistled at, beaten, raped, or murdered. That we deserve to be paid less than men, and that "women's work" in the home is less valuable than work that brings home a paycheck. That we must fit into the virgin-or-whore stereotype, and that we cannot make our own decisions about our bodies. In short, we reject the notion that we are second-class citizens.

My dream is to live in a world where the word *feminism* is unnecessary because it is obsolete, where its very definition has permeated our society and world, and where women and men are equally recognized and respected. We won't magically wake up to this world; we have to work to make it a reality. Embracing feminism and raising a voice against everyday sexism can be a humble start. We not only have to break the glass ceiling but smash the double standard that benefits men and the patriarchy with our bodies as the casualties.

One of the best professors I've ever had once said something that I've never forgotten. He proclaimed in front of a class of 25 students, without shame or apology, that he was a feminist. As the guys in the class shifted awkwardly in their seats, not quite sure how to react, I grinned and thought, "Finally." It was the first time I'd ever heard that word used by a man in a positive light. Surprise someone you know today, and redefine their notion of feminism. Explain that the human rights women benefit from in this country were hard-won and are not yet enjoyed by women everywhere. Explain that we still have a long way to go before we live in a world where women are truly safe, present, and accounted for. Explain that, yes, you're a feminist, and proud of it.

Allison Beltz is 24 and resides in the San Francisco Bay Area. She advises everyone to read Michelle Tea, Inga Muscio, and as many zines as possible.

The F-word

Feminism began as a term in France *(feminisme)* at the end of the 1800s coined by by Hubertine Auclert. It was then used in 1906, in an article by French suffragist Madeline Pelltier, that found its way to the United States. At that time, "women's liberationism" was the preferred term, but that started to get a bad name, so it was abandoned for "feminism."

What do you think of when you hear the word *feminism?*

"I think of a belief in equality."
—Kristen James, 23

"I reflect on my mother, who graduated from Smith in 1906, established herself as a working woman, married for love at age 40, and marched for a woman's right to vote."
—Laura Caldwell, 80

"I see the image of a woman standing exaggeratedly tall, her chest lifted, jaw pushed out, and I think of the frustration of having to overdo just to be seen, to be counted."

—Kristen Toedtman, 27

"I am more interested in what brings all of us together, regardless of gender, than I am in making more separation. I do believe that something is available with women that is unexpressed, but I think we need to be very careful in defining anything as feminine."

—Julie Gleeson, 53

"I think it needs to be redefined and expanded to include all of humanity."

—Audrey Hill, 34

"That there is an extraordinary mass of feminine menopausal energy that has just kicked in. 'We' will own more than 60 percent of the wealth in this country within 10 years, and we need to use this power and financial strength while this window is open."

—Mary-Jo Iacovino, 53

"I instantly think back to 1971, when I entered college. I felt as though I had been given permission to discard my bra forever, to be free from restraint."

—Deborah Charles, 51

"Humanism feels much more accurate to me. If one holds spiritual beliefs, that would mean that we are all a combination of both male and female characteristics (having lived both male and female incarnations), hence it would seem inaccurate, biased, and imbalanced to want to hold the singular views of either gender. Let's be human first."

—Colleen Adams

"I think it's a great concept, but the word carries dated connotations. I wish there were a new brand of feminism that would speak to young women, a brand that conveyed all that makes women strong without making them take on typically male characteristics like power and anger."

—Amy Chasen

"I wish there was a new word!"

—Kristan Lawson and Anneli Rufus

~ *Something to Think About* ~

A New Definition for the Word *Woman*

"Wife-man" is the partial etymological definition for the word origin of *woman;* however, all the definitions, perceptions, and ideas that society attributes to this one word, *woman,* could fill a book. I am 51 years of age. Notice I did not say "old." There are simply too many labels that can be attached to such a definition. Indeed, I am not "old" at all. "I" am a beginning. "I" am history. "I" am the present and the future. "I" am a multitude of life experiences. "I" am teacher, mother, wife, friend, nurse, doctor, therapist, housekeeper, nutritionist, economist, gardener, receptionist, secretary, taxicab driver, mechanic, architect, carpenter, electrician, firefighter, salesperson, and anything else that I must be in order to show to you the true meaning of me, "woman."

So the question is raised: What is a woman? Is there any one real definition? Can there be any simple answer to this profound question? Defined and given origin by man himself as the "wife-man," perhaps because a woman is a combination of man *plus* all that man seeks to be outside himself.

—Abby Caudle, 51

Feminism Would Have No Illusions

Cautious, careful people always casting about to preserve their reputation or social standards never can bring about reform. Those who are really in earnest are willing to be anything or nothing in the world's estimation, and publicly and privately, in season and out, avow their sympathies with despised ideas and their advocates, and bear the consequences.

—Susan B. Anthony

Recently I saw something that wiped the smile right off my face—the photos of American soldiers sadistically humiliating and abusing detainees in Iraq. These photos turned my stomach. But they did something else to me: They broke my heart. I had no illusions about the U.S. mission in Iraq, whatever exactly it is, but it turns out that I did have some illusions about women.

Here in these photos from Abu Ghraib, you have every Islamic fundamentalist stereotype of Western culture—all nicely arranged in one hideous image—imperial arrogance, sexual depravity . . . and gender equality. We don't know whether women were specifically ordered to participate in this kind of torture in order to humiliate Muslim men. All we know is that these women didn't say "No."

Maybe I shouldn't have been so shocked.

We know, too, that good people can do terrible things under the right circumstances. This is what psychologist Stanley Milgram found in his famous experiments in the 1960s. The women involved in Abu Ghraib are not congenitally evil people. They are working-class women who wanted an education and knew the military was the quickest way to get it. Once they got in, they wanted to fit in.

And I shouldn't be surprised either because I never believed that women are innately less aggressive than men. I have argued this repeatedly—once with the famously macho anthropologist Napoleon Chagnon. When he kept insisting that women were psychologically incapable of combat, I answered him the best way I could: I asked him if he wanted to step outside. . . .

I have supported full opportunity for women within the military, in part because—with decreasing access to college—it's one of the few options around for low-income young people.

I opposed the first Gulf War in 1991, but at the same time I was proud of our servicewomen and delighted that their presence irked their Saudi hosts.

Secretly I hoped that the presence of women would eventually change the military, making it more respectful of other people and cultures, more capable of genuine peacekeeping.

That's what I thought, but I don't think that any more.

A lot of things died with those photos.

The last moral justification for the war with Iraq ended with those photos. But there's another thing that died for me in the last couple of weeks: a certain kind of feminism or, perhaps I should say, a certain kind of feminist naïveté.

It was a kind of feminism that saw men as the perpetual perpetrators, women as the perpetual victims, and male sexual violence against women as the root of all injustice.

That was before we had seen female sexual sadism in action.

But it's not just the theory of this naïve feminism that was wrong. So were its strategy and vision for change. That strategy and vision rested on the assumption, implicit or stated outright, that women are morally superior to men.

Now, the implication of this assumption was that all we had to do to make the world a better place—kinder, less violent, more just—was to assimilate into what had been, for so many centuries, the world of men. We would fight so that women could become the generals, the CEOs, the senators, the judges, and opinion makers—and that was really the only fight we had to undertake. Because once they gained power and authority, once they had achieved a critical mass within the institutions of society, women would naturally work for change.

That's what we thought, even if we thought it unconsciously. And the most profound thing I have to say is that it's just not true.

What we have learned, once and for all, is that a uterus is not a substitute for a conscience and menstrual periods are not the foundation of morality.

This doesn't mean gender equality isn't worth fighting for for its own sake. It is. And I will keep fighting for it as long as I live. If we believe in democracy, then we believe in women's right to do and achieve whatever men can do and achieve, even the bad things.

It's just that gender equality cannot, all alone, bring about a just and peaceful world.

What I have finally come to understand, sadly and irreversibly, is that the kind of feminism based on an assumption of female moral superiority is a lazy and self-indulgent form of feminism.

Self-indulgent because it assumes that a victory for a woman—a promotion, a college degree, a right to serve alongside men in the military—is ipso facto—by its very nature—a victory for humanity.

And lazy because it assumes that we have only one struggle—the struggle for gender equality—when in fact we have many more. The struggles for peace, for social justice, and against imperialist and racist arrogance cannot, I am truly sorry to say, be folded into the struggle for gender equality.

Women do not change institutions simply by assimilating into them. But—and this is the "but" on which all my hopes hinge—a *certain kind* of woman can still change the world.

What we need is a tough new kind of feminism, with no illusions.

We need a kind of woman who can say *"No,"* not just to the date rapist or overly insistent boyfriend but to the military or corporate hierarchy within which she finds herself.

We need a kind of woman who doesn't want to be one of the boys when the boys are acting like sadists or fools.

And we need a kind of woman who isn't trying to assimilate but to infiltrate—and subvert.

We all have to become tough-minded activists for change because the entire feminist project is in terrible trouble worldwide. That project, which is minimally about the achievement of equality with men, is threatened by fundamentalisms of all kinds—Christian as well as Islamic.

But we cannot successfully confront that threat without a moral vision that goes *beyond* gender equality. To cite an old—and far from naïve—

feminist saying: "If you think equality is the goal, your standards are too low."

It is not enough to be equal to men when the men are acting like beasts.

It is not enough to assimilate. We need to create a world worth assimilating into.

BARBARA EHRENREICH is the author of *Nickel and Dimed* and the *New York Times* best-seller *The Worst Years of Our Lives*. She is a frequent contributor to *Time*, *Harper's Magazine*, *The New Republic*, *The Nation*, and *the New York Times Magazine*.

If Women Ruled the World

If women ruled the night time world
My love and I could dance
on moonlit paths in star struck peace
without a backward glance.

Our children could learn the zodiac
and phases of the Moon
and experience the equinox
without the dread of doom.

If women ruled the morning hours
we'd have a hearty breakfast
and hugs to send us on our way
to futures bright and so vast.

Our loves would live some extra years
without a heart attack
because the greed and driving pain
would be driven back.

If women ruled the mid-day hours
Our work would give us joys
Our days would create the communities' needs
to raise conscious girls and boys.

If women ruled the afternoon hours
We'd get a little rest
We'd have time to plan and organize
Our work could be our best.

If women ruled after-school hours
No kids would be alone
No hearts would be left broken
No questions left undone.

If women ruled the evening hours
The stress of day would melt
Each care could be examined
With every problem dealt.

If women ruled the dinner hours
All bellies would be filled
The garden would grow vegetables
The empty lots all tilled.

If women ruled the bedtime hours
Every person would tuck in
No sleeping under freeways
No taking it on the chin.

If women ruled the weeks and months
There'd be a place for men
To have a little elbow room
To come out of their den.

If women ruled the years ahead
We could save the oceans
We could make it safe for all
To manage their emotions.

When women find the strength to act
In focused long-term teams
And connect to each other in purpose
We will manifest our dreams.

Eleanor Oelsner, M.H., President of Healing Hearts World Retreats (a nonprofit for caregivers) has a private hypnotherapy practice in Atherton, California, and volunteers at Stanford/VA Hospitals as chaplain and reiki master.

ACKNOWLEDGMENTS

First and foremost, my gratitude to all the women who were courageous enough to step forward and share their passion, life experiences, and hopes for a better world. Thanks for taking a stand, investigating important issues, and taking the time to write from your heart. Your dedication to the changes you'd like to see in our world has become an inspiring invitation to all. And to Marie C. Wilson and Erin Villardi of The White House Project, thanks for your support and enthusiasm in working with us.

Without the editorial collaboration of Heather McArthur, I would have been swimming in a pile of essays long after the print date. Thanks for your amazing organizational skills, the ability to see the book as a whole, a second opinion whenever I needed one, and for finding an inspiring quote for every essay.

Thanks to the amazing team at Inner Ocean Publishing. First to Karen Bouris, publisher, for coming up with a fabulous title, brainstorming ideas, helping to determine the format, being persistent with the cover design, and all the other things that kept the book moving along. Your editorial contributions and direction, along with your belief that women's voices needed to be heard, kept me going. To Alma Bune, thanks for keeping every member of the team on track and for your invaluable research on sidebars. And to the rest of the team: Katie McMillan, John Elder, Dianna Grundhauser, Mark Kerr, Jane Evershed, Maxine Ressler, Valerie Sinzdak and Pam Suwinsky.

We would not have been able to get the word out or collect essays without the help of Mike Koenigs, who set up the Web site and spent many hours patiently explaining to me how things worked—I'm now a Webmaster! And to Trijnie Drenthe Wanders, who so creatively designed it.

My last and most important thanks go to my family, who support me every day, by making dinners, listening to my ideas, and understanding that mom has just one more hour of editing to go and then she can help with homework. Writing this book was like being a human filter with hundreds of women's ideas, pain, joy, frustration, and hope sifting through me and onto the page every day. Although I did notice those sidelong glances you gave each other at the dinner table when I bought up yet another important world issue we "had" to discuss, thanks for your willingness to engage in the process.

About the Editor

Sheila Ellison is the author of *How Does She Do It? 101 Life Lessons from One Mother to Another, The Courage to Be a Single Mother, The Courage to Love Again, 365 Ways to Raise Great Kids, 365 Days of Creative Play, 365 Games Babies Play, 365 Games Toddlers Play, 365 Afterschool Activities,* and *365 Foods Kids Love to Eat.*

She is the founder of the nonprofit organization Single Moms Connect, a parenting expert on radio shows across the nation, and a mother of four and stepmother of two. She has appeared on *Oprah!,* and her work has been featured in *O: The Oprah Magazine, Parenting, Family Circle, Ladies Home Journal, Glamour, Self,* the *New York Daily News,* the *San Francisco Chronicle,* and the *Oakland Tribune.*

Visit her online at www.CompleteMom.com.

Contributor Index

Join the Discussion

To continue the dialogue of issues presented in this book, to share ideas, to read new essays, or to find out about discussion groups in your area, go to www.IfWomenRuled.com.